The Kingdom Will Come Anyway

May 2020

To Gianni and Helen

With gratitude for our two families being able to share a rich friendship over many years

God's blessings...
Bob Luidens

The Kingdom Will Come Anyway

A Life in the Day of a Pastor—A Memoir

ROBERT J. LUIDENS

RESOURCE *Publications* · Eugene, Oregon

THE KINGDOM WILL COME ANYWAY
A Life in the Day of a Pastor—A Memoir

Resource Publications
An Imprint of Wipf and Stock Publishers
199 W. 8th Ave., Suite 3
Eugene, OR 97401

www.wipfandstock.com

PAPERBACK ISBN: 978-1-7252-6301-7
HARDCOVER ISBN: 978-1-7252-6302-4
EBOOK ISBN: 978-1-7252-6303-1

Manufactured in the U.S.A.   02/21/20

To the wonderful congregations of
First United Presbyterian Church in Lincoln, Kansas,
and
Altamont Reformed Church in Altamont, New York
With profound gratitude for the grace they have embodied and the
faith they have lived

Contents

Preface

IN THE LAST FEW years prior to my retirement from the pastorate, a beloved member of my congregation in upstate New York suggested to me that I should begin to make careful notes of various memorable experiences. She indicated I would benefit from those notes once I retired, since I would then be ready to write a book based on those experiences. I recall chuckling in response, indicating I had no aspirations about writing once retired. To the contrary, after having written well more than fifteen hundred sermons and eulogies, in excess of four hundred newsletter columns, innumerable reports for congregational meetings and committees and the like, once retired I was anticipating much reading, but little to no writing.

However, some six months into retirement a day came when with little forethought I sat down at the computer and began to draft one brief, recollective piece out of respect for my beloved, former parishioner. Two hours later I realized I was weeping. Writing had tapped not just memory, but blessing. Within a week's time thereafter, I had drafted two more such pieces. On each occasion I found myself tearing up, smiling, and having to confess that this was something I now had to do. Not for someone else, but for myself.

Each time I sat and composed an additional piece, other memories surfaced. Some were comic in nature. Others were tragic. A few were simply descriptive. Many were evocative of questions of faith, both answered and unanswered. But in every instance they reminded me of the unspeakable privilege and joy it had been to serve with two endearing congregations of fellow pilgrims and servants of Christ.

"The Kingdom will come anyway"—A Life in the Day of a Pastor is the product of some of those recollections and reflections. I share them with the hope they might open a window into the life of a pastor. But more importantly, I offer them with the prayer they might disclose some of the inspiring ways our loving creator molds and holds each and every one of us. I truly hope readers might find something within one or more of the following pieces that reveals a bit of the healing divine in the midst of the broken human.

Acknowledgments

THE HUMBLING TASK OF authoring a memoir has been pursued with the encouragement and counsel of many patient individuals.

Ellen Howie, dear friend and member of Altamont Reformed Church, was graciously persistent in her declaration that I would—even must—author a book in my retirement. I am indebted to her.

Glenn and Nancy Wagner, lifelong friends, gave insightful editorial advice and remained patient as sounding-boards. Their friendship is matchless.

Jennie Weber, a copy editor par excellence, was instrumental in helping me find both my voice and my style in written word. I am sincerely grateful.

Beth Carroll, Jill Russell, and Gordon Wiersma have proven to be warmly compassionate as my pastors in early retirement. They kindly read and commented on any number of anecdotes that found their way into the memoir. They have been wise and caring in their pastoral tone.

My family, including our three beloved children and my dear siblings, have cheered me on in the task of organizing and scribing memories and reflections from more than half a century. Not only have they been part of the story, they have enabled the telling of that story.

Finally, my wife has been an incomparable presence throughout our more than four decades of marriage. She has allowed me space to write, and has been the embodiment of soul-steadying love throughout. I could not have been in pastoral ministry, much less brought ministry memories to print, without her enouragement and solace.

ACKNOWLEDGMENTS

✳ ✳ ✳

The events embedded in this memoir are recounted with a desire to capture the truthful essence of each instance described. However, with only rare exception all of the individuals have been given pseudonyms, and incidental details are frequently altered in order to protect confidentiality, as appropriate. The author urges readers to derive benefit from the accounts without the necessity of identifying specific individuals described therein.

✳ ✳ ✳

Verses quoted in this memoir are from the New Revised Standard Version Bible, copyright 1989, by the Division of Christian Education of the National Council of Churches of Christ in the USA.

About the Author

THE AUTHOR WAS BORN in Iraq to missionary parents Edwin and Ruth Luidens, who raised him and his older siblings Don and Carol in Iraq, Lebanon, and New Jersey. Bob attended Hope College in Holland, Michigan, where he met classmate and future wife Mary Koeppe. Mary received her medical degree from the University of Michigan, and Bob received his master's degree from Yale Divinity School. Thereafter he was ordained into the ministry of Word and Sacrament within the Reformed Church in America.

Bob and Mary served for three years as pastor and physician in the farming community of Lincoln, Kansas. They then moved to upstate New York where Bob served for thirty-one years as pastor of the Altamont Reformed Church, while Mary pursued her advanced medical training as an endocrinologist and then served on the faculty of Albany Medical College. They retired from those positions and moved to Holland, Michigan, where they currently live.

Bob and Mary raised three children. Emily is a mathematics instructor in a community college, Karie is a writer and artist, and David is an orchestral percussionist. Bob and Mary delight in their two grandchildren, Katherine and Isaac, children of Emily and husband Matt Van Hook.

1

Desert Detour

IT HAPPENED AGAIN AND again. Both during my seminary years and my first decade in parish ministry, I would end up in discussion circles, attempting to introduce myself to new peers. And I would inevitably end up recounting the detour to the camp.

The various facilitators in those classroom and retreat settings back then would predictably invite each participant to "share a bit" about who we were and about what might have helped to shape us to that point in our lives. What would I typically feel drawn to describe? That springtime trip back when I was not yet ten years old.

My family was living in Beirut, Lebanon at the time. Dad and Mom decided it would be fitting for our family to spend our Holy Week vacation in Jerusalem, walking the Mount of Olives and visiting the traditional sites that define Maundy Thursday, Good Friday, and Easter Sunday.

The drive from Beirut to Jerusalem took us eastward to Damascus, Syria, and then southward through the arid plains that led to Amman, Jordan. From there we were to head westward into the West Bank of Jordan and ultimately up to the divided city of Jerusalem. The five of us squeezed into a taxi for hire in Beirut, with our typically jovial Lebanese driver at the wheel. Ahmed was a family favorite, having previously taken us on several day trips around Lebanon. My parents trusted him, and he seemed to enjoy being our chauffeur and tour guide.

But something unexpected and unsettling happened during that eight hour drive from the coastal city of Beirut to the holy heights of Jerusalem—something that shaped me, that transformed me.

As our trip entered into its southward leg from Damascus to Amman, driving through the desert-like plains of western Jordan, a heated conversation began to unfold in the front seat. It took me a few minutes to catch the essence of the quiet but intense exchange unfolding between Ahmed and my father. Dad was explaining that up ahead there was a right turn off of the road that Ahmed should take. That side road led westward, well off the main road to Amman, and into a Palestinian refugee camp.

Ahmed was clearly in disagreement with Dad's instruction. "Saheeb," I recall his saying to Dad, "thees ees noht goohd ahdea." Their quiet but intense debate migrated back and forth between English and Arabic. Sitting in the back seat of the taxi between my intrigued sister and my discomfited mother, I was fascinated if not distraught by the stridency of the low-voiced "discussion" up front. In retrospect, Ahmed was likely feeling genuine concern for our family's safety in the refugee camp. Westerners were few in number in the camp, and were understandably looked on by some therein with suspicion as being contributors to the dire circumstances they were now experiencing as refugees from their original homes.

But Dad prevailed. Clearly against his counsel to my father, Ahmed made the right hand turn. We drove some ten or fifteen minutes on a dirt-packed road, and arrived at the outskirts of a sprawling enclave in the desert. The camp was settled in 1948 by Palestinians who had fled their centuries-old homes during the carnage of the war that led to the establishment of the state of Israel. It was one of the many refugee camps that were now "home" to the otherwise homeless.

Ahmed drove us into the camp, through roughed out lanes that led to the buildings that housed United Nations workers. Those various internationals helped to provide the basic provisions necessary to keep the camp's tens of thousands of Palestinian refugees alive as they waited for the day, still not yet arrived more than a half century later, when they would be able to return to their original homes.

Dad exited the car and then tracked down and paid pastoral calls on several medical and missionary peers serving the camp's desperately needy residents. As he did so, Mom allowed my brother, sister, and me to move about a bit in close proximity to the car, in which Ahmed remained with a grim expression plastered on his face.

Finally Dad returned to the car. He proceeded to explain to us what we were seeing, but that regrettably too few people around the world cared to think about. Once back on the road he described how it was these thousands upon thousands of innocents, old and young alike, had become victims of a world gone mad with war and blind with apathy. I recall sitting in the back seat, twisting around as we passed through the camp's outskirts, looking at the hovels of the homeless and the faces of the forgotten. I felt a tight knot in my stomach. A bitter taste in my mouth. A gnawing pain in my heart.

I don't recall how or whether Dad said explicitly, "Do you see how this is wrong?" But I recall feeling that it was. Knowing that it was.

I'm convinced that was when I began to be shaped, transformed. A seed of discomfort was planted. A sense of injustice was incited. A desire for redemption was born.

Years later I queried my father about his decision to instruct Ahmed to take a detour that day on the Jordanian plains. He quietly acknowledged his intents were indeed twofold. First, he desired deeply to connect with his friends who were giving themselves in day to day service to the Palestinians whose lives were defined by that refugee camp. Second, he also yearned intensely to expose his three children to what our Palestinian neighbors were forced to endure as a result of dehumanizing political and religious decisions made hundreds and thousands of miles away.

Dad succeeded. At the same time he had embraced those in service within that camp, he purposefully had revealed to his offspring what human suffering looks like in its rawest form.

That detour to the camp still shapes me. Just as it was an event I felt compelled decades later to describe to my seminary classmates and my friends in ministry, it remains a moment in my life's pilgrimage that reminds me. That *re*-minds me.

In the days immediately after that detour, my family walked the Palm Sunday path down the Mount of Olives, sat beneath the trees of Gethsemane, and worshiped in the Garden of the Empty Tomb. And doing so was framed by that detour taken days earlier in the desert.

Such detours, I've come to believe, can lead us to truth. Can call us to compassion.

2

He Knew my Name on the Cross

I LAY ON THE top bunk, vaguely aware of the quiet snoring coming from the one beneath me. My freshman year roommate seemed always to fall asleep way before me, and that was happening again. But this time, there was no question as to why I was still wide awake.

It was Maundy Thursday, almost Good Friday according to the alarm clock on my desk. Earlier that evening I had attended the quiet Communion service in the college chapel, led by our deeply respected chaplain. Over previous years I had been to many such services on the Thursday evening of each year's Holy Week. This evening's version was not all that different from all of those I attended with my parents growing up. But now, lying in bed, something this time felt different. I hadn't yet put my spiritual finger on what, but I lay there mulling it over.

The readings and meditation during the service just a few hours earlier had recounted Jesus's meaning-laden Last Supper and unsettling prayer in the Garden of Gethsemane, followed by his arrest, trial, humiliation, and crucifixion. With the chapel lights extinguished, all of us had listened to Jesus's last words spoken before he died. Following the reading of his having "breathed his last," we exited the chapel in silence. I had walked back to the dorm with a handful of my freshman friends, and then had prepared for bed. Now lying awake, my roommate already in dreamland, I found myself revisiting the images embedded in that evening's scripture passages. As familiar as they all were, I found myself focusing on that of Jesus nailed to the cross. I envisioned him looking up on occasion, including when he was heard to pray for divine forgiveness on behalf of his executioners, and when he cried out in agony that he felt abandoned by his God. But I realized that I also pictured Jesus looking down from the cross, including when he addressed his mother and John, and when his thirst became overwhelming.

I mulled over those images, lying there on my bunk bed. Familiar, ages old statements of Christian conviction began to spin through my thoughts. "He died that we might *all* live." "He bore the sins of *all* of us." "He gave his life because of the love he had for *all* of the human family." I realized again and again the word "all" defined how it was I instinctively understood the object of Jesus's mission, of his self-sacrifice. That didn't surprise me. I had been raised within families, both nuclear and ecclesiastical, that rightly emphasized in the broadest terms what Jesus's life, death, and resurrection were all about: the salvation of all of broken creation, and all within it. I had been healthily steeped in a faith that urged me to emphasize the global blessings, rather than solely the personal benefits, of Jesus being the Lamb of God.

But there I lay on the top bunk, and, for whatever reasons that still elude me, the following began to stir within me. While Jesus hung upon the cross, looking down at his human sisters and brothers, he was giving his life not just for all of them and for all of us. He was giving his life for each *one* of us there at the foot of the cross, and even here, today, wherever we may find ourselves, including in a freshman dorm room on a college campus in North America. What began to stir within me, and even to astonish me, was that Jesus knew both the whole human family while he struggled for breath on Good Friday, but he knew me, as well. Me.

I recall my eyes watering as I lay there in the dark. I had been raised, gratefully, to recognize the cosmic, world-changing impact of Jesus's sacrificial life and love. But now, somehow, I began for the first time to recognize the personal, Bob-changing impact of that life and love. I still vividly remember whispering, "You knew *my* name, Lord? On the cross, while you were suffering unimaginable agony, you knew not just the names of everyone. You knew mine, as well!"

For a short while, lying still on my mattress, I struggled with whether it was fitting to forego, at least for the moment, the worldwide nature of

Jesus's sacrifice upon the cross. I struggled with whether it was unfitting to so personalize that sacrifice. But somehow, in ways that still betray the inadequacy of words, I knew that what I was grasping for the first time was as it should be: Jesus knew not just everyone on the cross, he knew me. Jesus gave himself not just for the world, but for Bob.

That's when the tears came. Not from narcissistic self-inflation, but from humbled gratitude. At age eighteen, I heard myself say, "Thank you." I let myself say, "Thank you for knowing me. Loving me. Personally."

In the four, nearly five, decades since lying on that bunk bed, tearing up with a smile on my face, I've never lost touch with the faith of my foremothers and fathers. I've held on, zealously, to the conviction that Jesus came to redeem the entire world, and that he will come to restore the whole of creation itself. But I've also allowed myself, with profound thankfulness, to proclaim to everyone that every *one* matters to that same Jesus, and that every *one* of us is known by, loved by, and embraced by him. That he knew the name of every single one of us as he looked both up *and* down while hanging on the cross.

3

Drafted into Ministry

FOR THE LIFE OF me, I did not know what to say. I stared at the gentleman and said nothing for a moment. I glanced to my right, catching the intrigued look on my pastor's face, and then turned back to the gentleman, saying, "I guess, sir, I've not really thought about going into the ministry before."

To which the member of the draft board said, "Well, it seems obvious to me you should."

Who could ever have guessed it would be there and then, for the first time ever, I would be urged to give serious consideration to entering into the ordained ministry?

Barely one year earlier, in 1971, I had done what all my fellow male high school classmates were lawfully expected to do. I had driven from my home in Teaneck, New Jersey, across the Hackensack River in search of the local Selective Service System (SSS) office. Recently turned eighteen years old, I had then registered for the draft. The war in Viet Nam was still raging, and the mandatory call-up of thousands upon thousands of young American men to serve in the military was in full swing.

But when I registered for the draft that late spring of 1971, I had checked off a box indicating I was applying for 1-O status, that of a conscientious objector. For several years I had struggled with the possibility I might be drafted into one of the nation's various services for the purpose of being trained to participate in military combat. My struggle led to a growing conviction I could not in good conscience carry a weapon and use it against another human. That conviction was rooted in my growing faith as a disciple of Jesus, whom I believed modeled and taught a life-giving alternative to violence, including and especially toward one's enemies.

After I registered that spring, I received standardized notice from the SSS office in Hackensack that my application for 1-O status would be considered only if and when my being drafted became a likelihood. Months passed. I began my undergraduate studies in Michigan, busying myself with all the college experience offered. Then, early in January of 1972 the day arrived when the SSS engaged in their annual public process of drawing numbers and dates from a bucket in Washington, DC. There were three hundred sixty-six dates, one for every calendar date, including February twenty-ninth. And there were three hundred sixty-six numbers. As each date was drawn, a number was then also drawn. My birth date matched with the number eight, which meant I would definitely be drafted into service the following calendar year.

I recall a sense of shock when I read in print my birth date paired with the number eight in the next day's newspaper. Along with those of my male peers who had similarly found their birth dates matched with numbers between one and one hundred, I found myself beginning to envision the impending disruption of my education and the required preparation of my written case in defense of my application for conscientious objector status.

I soon received the lengthy application instructions in the mail and noticed I would be scheduled to meet face to face with the SSS's local draft board in Hackensack that approaching summer. At the close of that meeting the draft board would vote on whether or not to grant me 1-O status, which in turn would determine whether I would be drafted into the Army or be directed into alternative service as a conscientious objector, more often than not as an orderly in a mental health institution.

Over the next several months I prepared a lengthy statement of faith as part of my application, and then secured several letters in support of that application. I sat for extended discussion, one on one, with my college's esteemed chaplain who, as I only later learned, had served with high distinction in the U.S. Army during World War Two. I corresponded with my pastor in New Jersey who graciously offered to accompany me to my summertime meeting with the draft board.

By late spring all of my application materials were in the hands of the draft board, whom I had yet to meet in person. They informed me by mail I was to report to them in late July for my face to face interview.

That evening arrived. My pastor kindly picked me up at my home, first pointedly coming into our living room to sit for a brief prayer with my parents and me. He and I then drove in relative quiet from my home to the SSS office in Hackensack. Once checked in by the receptionist, my pastor and I sat quietly waiting to be called into the draft board's meeting room. The appointed hour arrived and we were ushered in.

The group sitting around the large conference table included four men and one woman. They all stood and shook my hand. Two of the men were dressed in surprisingly casual attire. One of them, who looked no older than thirty, introduced himself as the chair of this particular local draft board.

I took my seat at one end of the conference table, with my pastor reassuringly sitting immediately to my right. I opened my personal copy of the application packet, ready to answer whatever questions would be forthcoming. The chair then said, "Robert, welcome." To my pastor he said, "Reverend, we're delighted you chose to accompany Robert for this meeting." My pastor expressed his appreciation for their allowance of his presence.

The chair then invited me to share in brief how and why I had come to the decision to apply for conscientious objector status. I could see that all five members of the draft board had copies of my application packet open on the table, but I had no idea as to whether or not they had read the contents. Presuming they had not, I revisited my statement of faith, which was required by law to be the underpinning of one's claim to be a conscientious objector.

I spoke for several minutes, during which all five listened intently. No one interrupted. When I concluded, I looked at the chair. He said, "Thank you, Robert." Then, rather than following up with a comment or question to me, he turned to the other four draft board members. "Anyone have any questions for Robert?"

I recall clenching my toes in anxious uncertainty about what might be unleashed by his invitation to his fellow board members. There was silence for three, four, maybe five seconds. Then one of the men, who was dressed in a three piece suit, said to the chair, "I have just one question." He then looked at me and said, "I'm somewhat surprised you haven't told us in your application that you're going to go into the ordained ministry."

I looked at him, somewhat confused. For the life of me, I did not know what to say. I stared at the gentleman and said nothing for a moment. I glanced to my right, catching the intrigued look on my pastor's face, and then looked back at the gentleman, saying, "I guess, sir, I've not really thought about going into the ministry before."

To which the member of the draft board said, "Well, it seems obvious to me you should."

Who could ever have guessed it would be there and then, for the first time ever, I would be urged to give serious consideration to entering into the ordained ministry?

I don't recall exactly what I said in response to his observation. Or was it advice? Regardless, I'm sure I said something intended to express appreciation for the kind of trust implicit in his statement. He then continued, in brief, to suggest the case I made for being declared a conscientious objector in the sight of the draft board was strong. The chair in turn proceeded to suggest the board could forego their typical movement into executive session prior to voting one way or the other. He took a vote in my presence, with all five raising their hands in affirmation of my application.

They then gathered up their papers, stood, and again shook my hand, indicating to me and my pastor we were free to leave. The chair noted I would receive the formal paperwork in due course.

Then my pastor and I drove home, a good bit earlier than I had anticipated.

I vividly remember describing the evening's meeting to my parents upon returning home. I particularly recall describing the one board member's statements about my considering the ministry. My mother teared up. My father nodded seriously. I don't recall that we discussed the statements about the ministry in much further detail. But I have no doubt in the least my parents had many discussions about it in the months and years that followed.

That fall I returned to college for my sophomore year. The ensuing January, when I was anticipating receiving my draft orders to prepare for my two years of alternative service as a conscientious objector, Secretary of State Henry Kissinger met in Paris with representatives of North Viet Nam's government. The upshot of their negotiations was an agreement to move toward cessation of hostilities. One of the immediate results of that agreement was the Nixon administration's decision to end the draft. Literally weeks, if not days, before I would have been ordered to prepare for draft service as a conscientious objector, that script evaporated. I ended up continuing my college career uninterrupted, graduating in four years.

By the end of the fourth year I began to feel a quiet call, a tender pull to give prayerful consideration to pursue training for the purpose of ordination into ministry.

How unpredictable, if not odd, that the one who first urged me to consider that vocational path was a member of the draft board in Hackensack, New Jersey. I never again met or spoke with that man. But I remain quietly indebted to him for his bold, affirming spirit. He embodies for me what it means to be a human instrument of the divine.

4

Consider the Lilies

"CONSIDER THE LILIES . . ." (Matthew 6:28) With those words Jesus as much as said, "Look carefully at what you see all around you. They are windows into what we need to see about our God and about our selves."

Apparently Jesus's followers frequently passed by lilies, but not surprisingly they had not seen them as windows. Likewise, on many occasions I had passed by feathers, but had failed to see them as windows into what I needed to see about my God and about myself. Until that day in the arboretum.

I had been aimlessly, even angrily, wandering those wooded acres of gardens that bordered the campus housing where my wife and I were living. I had just come from a daily pastoral support gathering that was part of my summertime ministry training. The gathering entailed a circle of five seminarians and a supervising pastoral mentor. Together we explored the challenges and demands of ministry. However, that morning the unexpected had unfolded. I had done as I was wont to do in that circle: inquire into the well-being of my peers, almost supplanting our mentor in that role. But then, to my unsettling dismay, one of those peers brazenly and bravely confronted me with her exasperation. She noted, with a quiet but blazing honesty, she felt that while I had come to know everything about everyone else in that circle, rarely if ever had I yet disclosed to them anything significant about myself.

I was so taken aback by her frank assessment that I shut down and shut up. In retrospect her diagnosis was spot on. But I was, in that moment, blind to the truth of her diagnosis. And I was deaf to the love that framed it. Rather, I felt accused, offended, and misunderstood. After a few minutes of sputtering, immobilized reactivity, I rose and announced I was done. Through. Gone.

I left, mid-meeting, mid-stream. I headed off to the nearby arboretum, licking my wounds in self-absorbed pity.

I honestly don't recall how long I wandered the woods and gardens, but it was long enough that I had time to mutter again and again, "They don't know me. How can they accuse me, if they don't know me?" The wandering and muttering continued until, with no particular forethought, I found a tree under which to plant myself.

In retrospect, that tree hearkened back to the proverbial bush on the eastern outskirts of Nineveh and under which dear old Jonah chose to plunk himself in unbridled irritation once he realized Yahweh was a God of shocking grace rather than punitive judgment (see Jonah 4). Just as that Old Testament era prophet had grumbled in the shade of his tree of discontent, so now did I.

And that's when I saw it. A feather. A blue jay's feather. I mutely stared at it, lying there in the grassy shade of my tree of discontent. And, for whatever divine reason, I reached out and picked it up.

"Consider the lilies . . ."

I looked at the feather, spinning it between my thumb and middle finger, still nursing my pain and irritation from an hour or two earlier. That's when I saw it. That's when I noted what I had probably gazed upon many times before—when I had happened upon blue jay feathers lying about—but what I had not yet recognized. That feather, with a beautiful mix of blues lining its curved edge, was as gray and plain-looking as possible everywhere else. The feather's blue was only on its edge that is visible, lying feather upon feather, to the rest of the natural world. But the vast majority of that feather was not blue, but gray and plain.

Then it hit me: a blue jay, with all its spectacular beauty, can fly because of feathers that are, for all practical purposes, primarily gray and plain. Ordinary. Just as God fashions them to be. Up to that point, I realized, I had always thoughtlessly presumed a blue jay's feathers are not just blue edgewise, but blue everywhere. Not so.

Now I realized, with a frown still on my forehead but a tinge of a smile beginning to curl my lips, that those feathers are unarguably gray, not blue. Take away the gray portion of those feathers, and the bird won't be able to fly. In fact, take away the gray, and the bird will never even survive the cold.

"Consider the lilies. Look carefully at what you see all around you. They are windows into what we need to see about our God and about our selves."

That blue jay feather? It was a mirror, blessedly given me by my shockingly gracious God. I suddenly saw myself in that feather: beautifully blue on the edge, and—not but, but *and*—gray and plain otherwise.

Oh.

This is how you, Lord, have fashioned me, your blue jay feather? Blue *and* gray. Beautiful *and* plain. And you are well pleased with that fashion?

Oh.

Ohhhh.

Thank you.

I recall a chill, or maybe a warmth, coursing through me, body and soul. It became crystal clear: I can show the gray and plain to my friends, my peers, my neighbors. I can reveal what is not blue, and celebrate the not-blue, because the not-blue is good. Is God-colored. Is God-loved.

The following morning, at the appointed time I returned to be part of the pastoral support gathering. Upon my arrival, my peers looked up in surprise and evident relief that I had returned to be part of the circle. Part of them. They embraced me with the same love that had, in truth, given birth to their confronting honesty of the day before. Then, as part of that circle of grace, I showed them the feather. I showed them my self. The one they so much wanted to see and to know and to embrace, as gray and blue as each of them was.

As each and every one of us is.

"Consider the lilies . . ."

5

You're Why

I WAS SITTING ON the springtime grass of a little hill, only a stone's throw from the seminary chapel. And I was saying to myself, or more truly to Jesus, "Oh, that's why I really am a believer. *You're* why."

Less than an hour earlier, in a large lecture hall with well more than a hundred other divinity school students, I had sat listening intently to our professor expound on the essence of his book. Henri Nouwen, esteemed worldwide for his reflections on the inner, spiritual life, was thinking aloud about his core emphases embedded in *The Wounded Healer*, written and published globally nine years earlier.

Born and raised in the Netherlands, Henri had been trained in psychology and ordained a Catholic priest. Now on the seminary faculty, his class sessions broke all norms. They were not lectures. They were spiritual experiences. He would typically begin each hour session with a time of prayer, during which silence well superceded words. But when he spoke, be it in prayer, or most remarkably while reading a text from scripture, it was always at a snail's pace. Henri didn't know how to rush. Or more to the point, he knew how to take his time, and in doing so he modeled for his students how to slow down. How to listen, to watch.

That morning Henri had proposed to us, as he had in *The Wounded Healer*, that the model for us as aspiring pastors not surprisingly was, and should always be, Jesus. In his distinctive Dutch accent, he declared, *"But— but* (five second pause) *ve too easily forget dhat Jesus* (five second pause) *vas a vounded man.* (ten second pause, with pens now put down, note taking over) *Dhe reason dhat people listened* (five second pause) *and followed* (five second pause) *vas dhat Jesus never hid his vounds.* (ten second pause) *Dhis ve forget.* (ten second pause) *Dhis ve each must remember* (five second pause), *especially vhen ve are pastors to our sheep.* (ten second pause) *Vhen you are dheir pastor, dheir shepherd, dhey vill need you* (five second pause) *to show dhat you, too, are as vounded as dhey are.* (ten second pause) *Dhen dhey vill know dhat you can understand dhem.* (ten second pause) *Dhen dhey vill know dhat you truly love dhem, just like Jesus loves dhem."*

Henri's point was transparent, unarguable, and utterly transforming. He was making clear what my intellect already knew, but which my heart hadn't yet come close to fathoming. Jesus, whom I had learned about in family, catechism, and worship, had always been to me the embodiment of perfection, sin-free thought, and unimpeachable action. But that picture of Jesus was only two dimensional. It revealed who he is, but from a distance. I had always admired, even been awed by, that Jesus. But I hadn't come to know him as someone who understood me. Why *would* I, quite frankly? Why would I allow him to draw close, with his glowing perfection, when I knew his proximity would bring to glaring light my own imperfection?

Now, however, a different, almost shocking picture of Jesus was being painted by this Dutch mentor. In his quiet but powerful manner Henri was adding a third dimension to my picture of Jesus. He was insisting we see the real Jesus as a wounded man. Wounded, just as every other human has ever been wounded.

Henri's point was not original with him. He was, to the contrary, lifting up that easily overlooked image from scripture itself. Henri was simply unearthing what was always rooted in Jesus's story: his full, unadulterated humanity, with the same vulnerability to sorrow, loneliness, and pain that defines the experience of every one of us in the human family. But he was rightly unearthing it for the likes of me, who for any number of reasons had imaged the Nazarene as sinless, but distant, too. As free of imperfection, but innocently incapable of empathizing with the suffering of the imperfect.

In his incomparably simple and profound way, Henri was coaxing us to add the third dimension to our picture of the Nazarene. *But we too easily forget that Jesus was a wounded man. The reason that people listened and followed was that Jesus never hid his wounds. This we forget. This we each must remember, especially when we are pastors to our sheep. When you are their pastor, their shepherd, they will need you to show that you, too, are as wounded as they are. Then they will know that you can understand them. Then they will know that you truly love them, just like Jesus loves them.*

Now, an hour later, I was sitting on the springtime grass of a little hill, only a stone's throw from the seminary chapel. And I was saying to myself, or more truly to Jesus, "Oh, that's why I really am a believer. *You*'re why." A picture was taking shape within me, although now it was three dimensional. Jesus was at the center of the image, and he was leaning close to the ear of the divine figure sitting on the eternal throne of grace. In the picture I noticed Jesus's brow. It still bore the scars from the thorny crown. And I noticed Jesus's wrists. They still bore the nail wounds. And I noticed Jesus's eyes. They still revealed the sadness he felt just as the cock crowed. And, in that same living image, that's when I heard Jesus whisper. His hushed voice was both intense and compassionate. I heard him say, "Let me tell you about Bob. Let me help you to understand him and all that he has been through, and is going through right now."

That's when Jesus became my closest friend, the one I knew would always understand me. That's when I realized that I would never again feel alone in my pain. Would never again feel isolated in my sorrow. Would never again feel lonely in my troubles.

That's when I decided to be more like the one who truly understands me. Who truly loves me.

That's when I decided never again to hide my wounds.

6

Grace at the Table

I SUSPECT THAT EVERY young pastor leaves the ivy covered halls of theological education with at least one goal in mind. She or he heads off to the first ministry setting with the goal of embodying God's grace for a congregation who are desperately in need of learning what that grace is all about. Then, to the amazement of the newly ordained pastor, she or he discovers that the congregation is already primed to display said grace to the minister newly in their midst.

Such was the case for me. All it took was a moment of unanticipated calamity and a month of anxiety-filled uncertainty, followed by that grace unspoken but undeniable.

The calamitous moment unfolded as I stood behind the Communion Table on the Sunday, just days after arriving in town, when I would lead for my first time the celebration of the Lord's Supper. I had studiously memorized the liturgy, calculating that I had anticipated each and every possible sacramental twist and turn that might come my way during that first Communion service.

But, as prepared as I thought I was, nope.

That morning there were three women serving as the volunteer team who had carefully prepared all of the elements of Bread and Cup for this momentous service with the brand new minister from "back east" in Connecticut. They had decided to fill to the *brim*, mind you, the chalice that I was tasked with lifting during the liturgy, and from which I was then to drink while the assembled congregation drank from their own miniscule plastic cups. Having never to that point ever drunk from a chalice, but only from those tiny little cups, I was ill prepared, to put it mildly. Accustomed over previous years to taking those small cups and tossing their contents into my mouth with a Nike-like swoosh, I now did the same with the chalice. The same chalice that was so kindly filled to the top by the thoughtful threesome. Before I knew it, I was gagging on a mouthful of Welch's. And in that same moment I realized the juice that hadn't found its way into my mouth was now washing freely down my brand new preaching robe.

In an instant I realized there was good news, and there was bad news.

The good news was the robe still had on it the water-resistant protective coating applied in gracious measure by the company from which my mother-in-law had ordered it as my ordination gift. The upside: that purple juice sluiced straight down and off of the robe. Not a stain would remain on that wonderful attire.

However, there was bad news, as well. Really bad news. What juice ran down and off the robe ran straight onto the brilliantly white cloth on the Table. The cloth that had very recently been bleached, pressed, and caringly blanketed on the Table.

Uh-oh.

Though it all happened in a matter of seconds, I still remember it vividly. Since the vast majority of parishioners were still tossing the juice up and into their own mouths, heads bent backwards and eyes heavenward, hardly anyone had yet noticed the disaster unfolding up front. But there were two exceptions. In the front pew on their own, directly in front of the Table, sat a couple of adolescent girls. They saw. And they let loose with a muffled laugh that made it clear they were now witnesses to an event that would require recounting to all of their friends as soon as the newbie culprit had intoned the service's benediction.

What's a young pastor to do under these less than fortunate circumstances? Well, pray, of course. Standing there behind the Table, trying to catch my breath as the juice coursed down my robe and smack dab onto the white cloth, I gasped, with as much sacred dignity as possible, "Let us pray."

Well.

The rest of the service sped by. With Communion behind—or in front of?—me, and the service finally brought to a sweaty conclusion, I walked to the back of the sanctuary in order to greet my new flock. Remarkably, not a word was said about The Spill. Not even from the two young teens who came through the line and smiled knowingly at their fool of a new pastor.

I headed home for lunch, recounting the scene to my ever-patient wife. It was only in doing so that I spoke the unspeakable: "The cloth on the Communion Table! Oy! I've stained it beyond measure with the juice poured so generously by the same women who by now have found it and are faced with the impossible job of nursing it back to clean health!"

The next four weeks crept by. I knew that the next Communion Sunday was coming. None too soon, but coming nonetheless, no matter how much I fervently prayed the Return of our Lord would arrive first.

That's when and how I learned about grace.

This foolish young pastor, who thought it *my* responsibility to disclose the mysterious nature of God's grace to this poor congregation, discovered the congregation to be the true teachers par excellence. Early in the morning on that next Communion Sunday I stole with caution into the sanctuary, unsure what condition I would find the Table, its cloth, and the chalice. To my utter astonishment, I discovered the Table to be beautifully prepared. The cloth was even whiter than it had been on the previous Communion Sunday. The chalice? Filled. Well, not to the brim. Not even close. It had juice in it, but only in an amount that matched that of all of the little juice cups in the trays sitting on that white cloth.

And guess what? Not a word spoken to this young pastor by those three amazing women. Rather, in their quiet way they had chosen to be models of grace. They had cleaned up after their pastor, and then had enabled their pastor to serve.

If ever there were living witnesses to the grace, love, and divinely good humor of our Lord, they were embodied by those three women. And, truth be told, by the two smiling teens once again sitting in the front pew, as well.

7

Appetite for Listening

NORMALLY THE MEAT, POTATOES and veggies on my dinner plate would disappear fairly quickly. But not that Sunday noon. No, not that Sunday noon. "And for good reason," I was telling myself distractedly. For the third Sunday in a row, it had happened. I just had to be curious—vain, maybe?—and actually ask the folks, "How so?"

I was only a month and a half into my first pastorate. I had been in the pulpit five, maybe six times, and had appreciated the weekly comments after worship while greeting the parishioners as they departed through the main door. "Good sermon, Pastor Bob." "I really liked your message this morning, Bob." "Thanks, Reverend. Inspiring sermon today."

But as complimentary as those words were, curiosity—or vanity—got the better of me. I decided to inquire. "How so, Florence?" "How so, Lyle?" I was really interested. I wanted to glean what it was that was striking home, so I could be attentive to the real needs of my parishioners as I forged into this new vocation of preaching.

Then, over the course of those three Sundays in a row, Florence, Lyle, and several other wonderful souls stood in the doorway of the church and answered my question. They explained to me exactly what they had taken from my sermons. What they heard that was so meaningful, so helpful.

And as each took the time to do exactly what I invited them to do, I stood there in quiet confusion. Well, actually, in unsettled irritation. Because it was becoming jarringly clear to me I had landed in a church community where no one knew how to listen to a sermon. Each and every one described to me what she or he had "heard" while I delivered my masterfully crafted meditations. And not one of them was describing what I was certain I had said just thirty minutes earlier. Not one. Rather, each described being touched by one thing or another I knew I couldn't locate in my manuscript even if I spent eternity scouring through the text.

Now it wasn't as though their descriptions were pithy, or trite, or frivolous. No, they were detailing substantive issues in their lives. Loneliness. Doubt. Fear. You name it, they were describing it to me.

But how, I silently asked myself while standing in the doorway of the church building those three successive Sundays, *how* were they hearing this stuff? It wasn't in my manuscript and what I had so succinctly proffered from the pulpit.

So that third Sunday noon I had lost my appetite, and it wasn't just for the roast beef, mashed potatoes, and corn on my plate. It was for my vocation. Or maybe it was for my parishioners, who seemed disappointingly to be not very skilled at listening to their eager, albeit fresh out of seminary minister.

That's when my saintly wife did what she's done countless times over the four decades of our marriage. Mary asked me, "What's up? You seem bothered." Humph. I vaguely recall shrugging, not wanting to talk, yet *really* wanting to talk. "You okay?" she quietly persisted.

"Sort of, but kinda not." She waited quietly. I put my fork down. I looked at her, feeling so, so sorry for myself. Poor me. "They don't listen very well," I mumbled.

"Who?" Mary asked.

"All the members of the church."

"What do you mean they don't listen very well?"

So I explained to her, with pathos-filled, dramatic flourish, how the very same folks who said they had appreciated my sermons these past three Sunday mornings, were making it very clear they hadn't heard a word I had said. She invited me to clarify. I did, in full, self-pitying detail.

That was when she was supposed to put her compassionate hand on my shoulder and comfort my wounded ego. But instead, bless her, she said in a fairly matter of fact manner, "Apparently you don't get it, do you."

Huh? I stared at her, wondering if it was happening again: now even my wife didn't know how to listen to me! "What don't I get?" I managed to ask.

"That each of us sitting in the pews is meant to hear what each of us needs to hear, and that differs from person to person." She stopped. Then I stopped, too, and finally began to listen. "You don't really think that the specific words that *you* happen to speak from the pulpit are the very words that each of *us* needs to hear, do you? We're meant to hear what God wants us to hear. You have the task of helping us in that direction. But then we each need to hear what *God* is saying, not you."

She stopped again, and then continued, "It's evident that you're already a pretty good preacher, Bob. Your parishioners are telling you that. Right?" I slowly nodded, just beginning to understand what I thought I had come to understand through five years of theological training prior to my recent ordination. "Your sermons are fine, considering you're brand new at it." She smiled. "And I'm sure they'll get even better as the years go by." She looked me in the eye. "And they're good because they're already helping the rest of us listen to God." She stopped. "Yes, of course, to you. But more importantly, to God."

Oh. Of course.

Oh! Of *course*! In that moment I determined to do what my beloved parishioners had already been doing far better than I. I, too, began to listen to God, who in that moment was speaking gently and unarguably through Mary.

I picked up my fork and began to eat. My appetite had begun to return.

8

Like Father, Like Son

"HEH," CHUCKLED MURPHY. "LIKE father, like son." He smiled at us, betraying he had figured out something truly comical about us. My Dad and I grinned dumbly back at him, not in the least appreciating the humor of the moment.

Murphy began to explain. "Your son here," he said, hooking his thumb in my direction, "asked me the same question a few weeks back."

I quickly and silently reviewed for myself the visit in question. Murphy and his quiet wife Velma had invited me out to their farm, some six miles from town. I had driven alone from the church building, relishing the gently rolling plains of northern Kansas along the way. On my arrival at the farm, but before enjoying the fresh apple pie that Velma was cooling on the kitchen table, Murphy had directed me to follow him to the barn. There he instructed me to climb up on his tractor and to hang on to the back of his driver's seat, into which he then planted himself. For the next hour he drove me around their expansive farm, introducing me to his widely scattered cattle and his lush fields of wheat and sorghum. We had carried on a bouncy conversation, our loud voices competing with the grumbling John Deere engine.

As I now replayed my memory of that illuminating, if not teeth rattling, jaunt around the back forty, I realized I had indeed back then posed the same question my Dad had just now asked Murphy while sitting in their comfortable parlor.

Dad was visiting from his home back in New Jersey. Murphy and Velma, knowing he was coming, had extended an invitation for me to bring him to their farm in order to give him a warm Kansan welcome. Having accepted, I had now driven with Dad back to the same farm house. After a brief backyard vista-viewing offered to Dad, the four of us were now chatting amiably in their parlor. That's when Dad asked the question. "So, how many acres of land do you farm, Murphy?"

"Heh," chuckled Murphy. "Like father, like son." His eyes scrunched up a bit. He smiled. As did we, though not sure what the joke was.

"Oh?" said Dad amicably.

"Yup. Like father, like son." My stomach began to churn just a bit. He continued. "Last month your son here came out and we took a tractor ride around the farm."

"Yes, Bob told me about that." Dad nodded in my direction, and both of us grinned again. Gratefully Dad added, "And he said it was a wonderful experience."

"Glad to hear it," said Murphy. Velma nodded in agreement. After a pregnant pause, he explained, "Well, you see Reverend Luidens, while we were ridin' around the farm, Pastor Bob here asked me the same question you just asked me. He asked, 'How many acres do you have? How many head o' cattle do you have?'" Murphy looked at me, then at Dad again. "Same question, basically, that you just asked me."

Dad nodded, continuing to smile. I could almost read Dad wanting to say, "Just being interested, Murphy." But thankfully he held his tongue, waiting for Murphy to continue, which Murphy did. "Well, Reverend, I'll answer your question, same's I did with your son. Velma and I have two hundred and fifty acres planted, and some sixty head o' cattle." He smiled again. "I'm telling you all o' that, just like I told your son here, 'cause I know those numbers don't likely mean nothin' to you." We nodded, even more confused than a moment earlier. "Y'see, Reverend, your askin' a farmer how much land he owns, or how many cows he has, is kinda like them askin' you, 'How much money you got in your bank account?'"

He stopped, his eyes fairly glowing with delight. "But I knew, with both your son before, and now with you: I could tell you those numbers, and you'd still have no idea what the numbers really mean."

Dad and I looked at each other, then back at Murphy. Then at Velma, who was chuckling now, right along with her beloved Murphy.

"Like father, like son," he said again, clearly barely able to contain himself for the simple humor this pair of well-meaning, city-slicker Easterners was providing them. Providing them because of our total naiveté, wrapped in pastoral care, with a great big dollop of look-alike, father-and-son comedy on top.

We all nodded together, with Dad and his cookie-cutter son now recognizing the comic relief that we were providing dear Murphy and Velma.

With that all clarified, Velma spoke up for the first time. While serving us enormous slices of warm, peach pie, she said to no one in particular, "'Course we farmers don't have to ask how many acres or how many cattle our neighbors have. We all know what everyone else has—and is worth—just by lookin'." And as she sat back down in her chair, she displayed a little curl of a grin. She glanced knowingly at her beloved husband, and noted just loudly enough for all of us to hear, "But we would never admit it. Never."

9

Present and Accounted For

IT WASN'T JUST THAT I was a bit offended all six men fell fast asleep within the first two minutes of my sermons those three successive Sundays in February. It was that the six wives, sitting alongside of their husbands, seemed almost oblivious—seemed as if they didn't even know, much less care, that their Sunday best-dressed spouses were snoozing away during their young pastor's finely honed homilies.

By the time the third Monday that month rolled around, I happened to cross paths with one of those dear women. Just inside the door of the post office, I bumped into Florence, whose husband Fred was one of the guilty six from the day before. "Good Monday morning to you, Florence," I offered when we caught each other's eye. She was fiddling with the key to her mail box, so I saw fit to sidle up to her, real pastor-like. "How are you folks?"

"Fine, Pastor Bob. How about you and Dr. Mary?"

"Doing well, Florence. Thanks for asking." A slight pause, while I weighed the moment. The opportunity. Why not, Bob? Go ahead and ask her. "Say, Florence. I was thinking yesterday afternoon. About Fred."

She turned to face me, mail now in hand. "Yes?"

"Well, I hope he's okay." Another pause. "Yesterday morning I noticed he was having some difficulty staying awake for the latter part of the service. It struck me that had happened the previous two Sundays." Another pause. "Is he okay?"

Florence, gracious woman that she was, smiled a bit. Gracious and astute. "You noticed he's fallen asleep a few times lately, have you?"

With a silly grin I said, "Now that I've been in the pulpit for six months, I've discovered I can see all kinds of things from up there. Things I never saw before."

"I see," said Florence. Another pause. "Well, I guess maybe I ought to fill you in about Fred, and about the other farmers who manage to get to worship every Sunday, including in the dead of winter." And with that, Florence spelled it out for this young pastor who clearly knew practically nothing about the real lives of his amazing parishioners.

Florence described how Fred, every Sunday morning, rose early enough to tend to their cattle prior to coming into town for 9:30 a.m. worship. During the coldest stretch of mid-winter, she explained, when the temperature fell into the single digits and below, and when the westerly wind blows frightfully out in the pastures, the cattle understandably wander into culverts in order to keep from freezing to death. Fred, along with all the other decent farmers who care for their charges, would rise about 3:30 a.m., put on four layers of winter clothing, and head out to the barn. There Fred would take thirty minutes to load silage—food for his herd—onto the trailer behind his tractor, and then would head out in the total dark into the hundreds of acres of grazing land in search of those scattered, freezing cattle. Hunting until he found every last one of them, he would drop silage for each one, ensuring as well that all the water troughs scattered about had their thick coat of ice chopped up in order to allow the cattle to drink.

Florence explained how all of that would take two to three hours, after which Fred would return the tractor and its now emptied trailer to the barn. He would wander back into the farm house, remove his layers of protective garb, and head upstairs for a hot shower. He would then dress, putting on the Sunday suit that Florence by then had laid out on their bed. Breakfast followed. Not Rice Krispies, but eggs and ham, with a large side of hash browns. Thereafter, the two of them would load into the pick-up and drive the thirty minutes into town in order to be in their regular pew well before the young pastor strutted into the sanctuary, robed and fresh-faced.

Florence continued. She pointed out helpfully, to her now humbled audience of one, the sanctuary is always comfortably warm, compared to the frigid air blowing outside. She concluded, "So by the time we get around to listening to your helpful sermons, Fred and the other farmers in church have been up and working for six hours. In the dark, all alone, making sure the beef the rest of us enjoy for noontime dinner doesn't first perish due to the elements."

With that she smiled. Or maybe frowned just a bit. "So you can probably see why all of us wives don't mind if our husbands can't stay awake for the sermon. The fact they're there, in the pews, dressed and all, is right and proper." Another pause.

"Florence," I stammered. "I'm not sure what to say, other than 'Forgive me.' I had no idea."

"'Course you didn't, Pastor Bob. How would you." Not a question. A statement. "But now you know."

With that I stumbled to the post office door, holding it wide open for Florence as she headed to her car. Back to the farm. Back to be there for, and with, her amazing husband.

Later in my study, processing what Florence had brought to light, it hit me. Over the course of those three previous Sundays in question, more than a handful of regular worshipers had been absent. Not one was a farmer from the outer parts of the county. The absentees were pretty much all folks who lived in town, some just a few blocks from the church. I had run into at least a couple of them during that stretch, at the post office, of course, and each one had noted this bitter cold, with the wind and drifting snow, had made it too treacherous to get to worship.

"Hmm," I thought.

The following Sunday, when Fred and Florence came through the line at the back of the sanctuary following the benediction, I looked both of them in the eye. I said, "It is a humbling privilege to be your pastor."

Florence nodded, smiled, and quietly took her husband's arm as they headed to their pick-up.

10

Pulpit Surprise

I was already nervous, given that morning's text from Exodus: "You shall not commit adultery." (Exodus 20:14) But the nerves instantaneously turned to silent panic when I looked down and found "2" typed at the top of the page sitting on the pulpit. "Not possible!" my mind screamed to itself. "Not possible!"

But not to be too crass about it, the show must go on. So I started.

Not more than two hours earlier I had stood at the same pulpit, with the sanctuary devoid of anyone else. As was my routine, now a full two years into my first parish, I had rehearsed my sermon enough times up through that early Sunday morning that I was able to deliver the message with only occasional glances down at the manuscript. But that manuscript remained on the pulpit, available for those moments while preaching when I would take a peek at it to ensure I was staying on course.

Satisfied that all was readied for the 9:30 service, I headed home for a light breakfast with my wife, and then returned at 9:00, once again ensuring all was in place, including that treasured manuscript. A few minutes thereafter, in walked the four lay people who had kindly agreed to provide liturgy assistance that particular Sunday, which the denomination had entitled "Laypersons' Sunday." In an effort to honor the intent of the occasion, I had earlier solicited volunteers to help with scripture readings and prayers. Four folks kindly stepped forward, including Mildred.

Mildred was a retired school teacher, widowed and in her eighties. She was, to use a Kansan expression favored by several farmers in the congregation, "a ball of fire." Voluble, and self-admittedly comfortable with the spotlight, Mildred fit the bill. I had asked her to read the Old Testament texts for that morning's sermon. They were again from Exodus, as had been the case each of the previous six Sundays.

On the earlier request of one of the women's fellowship groups, I had embarked on a sermon series about the Ten Commandments: ten sermons in ten weeks. This Sunday, being week seven, brought us to the commandment I had been less than enthused about having to address. Twenty minutes on adultery? Please. God had made it quite clear: don't do it. What? Did that take more than three seconds to cover? And I had another nineteen minutes and fifty-seven seconds to fill? But remarkably that week I had managed to find plenty to massage into what was going to be a masterful reflection on why God thought adultery worthy of prohibition. The result: twelve pages, double spaced, with each page numbered at the top.

Which brings us back to that moment of, uh, unadulterated panic.

Earlier in the service Mildred had read the assigned readings, ending with the one verse that would now be the focal point of our congregational reflection: "You shall not commit adultery." Predictably, she read it with conviction, with intensity. Then she collected her Bible and personal papers from the pulpit, hobbled down the aisle to her seat in the third pew on the left, and sat down.

I in turn rose from the pastor's chair, walked solemnly to the pulpit, and invited all to join me in a prayer asking God to guide our ensuing reflections. Little did I know how significant a prayer that truly was. Because, upon pronouncing "Amen" with appropriate solemnity, I did as I was accustomed at that point in time every Sunday morning: I looked down at the opening words on the top page in order to dive into my well-honed text. And I saw this:

the wilderness, after having passed through the Red Sea and escaped

I stared in speechless confusion. I knew that the first words, as they had been the previous six Sundays, were to be those of the specific commandment in question. But where were the words of the seventh commandment?

That was when I looked at the small number at the top of the page. And I saw "2." Not "1," which was supposed to be there. "2."

I almost said aloud, "Not possible!" I was sincerely tempted to blurt out, "Who took page one?" But my grey matter resisted just enough that I simply stood there, mute. For at least three or four seconds. Or was it three or four hours?

What to do? Well, start, Bob. Which is what I did. "You shall not commit adultery," I declared. I probably shouted it out, given the angst that had now swept through me. A second time: "You shall *not* commit adultery." The congregation listened with rapt attention. *Preach it, Pastor Bob*! I stopped for a second or two. Then, thankfully, the words began to come. I started to recall what I had so carefully typed on line two of page one. And then lines three, four and five. All the way to page two of the manuscript. All the way to the wilderness, where God had led the Israelites after their having passed through the Red Sea and escaped from Pharaoh's army.

By the time I had worked all the way to and through page twelve, and ended with, "Please pray with me," I was sure that *no* one in that congregation would dare contemplate adultery again. At least for the next twenty-four hours.

Which was the duration of time it took for Mildred to phone me at the church that Monday morning, asking if she could stop by for a moment. Ten minutes later in she hobbled, waving off my invitation to sit. "Good day to you, Bob."

"And to you, Mildred. How are you?"

"Well, a wee bit embarrassed," she said. "I think I have something of yours." With that, she handed me a severely folded piece of paper. Page one. "Found this in my things when I got home yesterday. Didn't know what it was at first. Then I read it and realized what I had done." She gave me a wry smile and announced, "Guess you knew enough about adultery that you didn't even need the first page of your sermon." Her eyes danced about just a bit, and then: "Best be gettin' on."

"Thanks, Mildred. I appreciate your returning this to me. I admit to having been a bit confused when I found it missing yesterday morning."

"Well, it didn't show, Bob." She moved toward the door, ready to make her escape. But without turning, she then said over her shoulder, "Guess you should know I've told all my friends about what happened. They all think it's kinda comical you knew so much about adultery."

With that Mildred departed, leaving behind her young pastor chuckling, just as, in all likelihood, so many of her beloved pupils had done over the years.

11

Not in Kansas Anymore

"WELL, I'M CERTAINLY NOT in Kansas anymore," I mumbled discretely to myself, while outwardly smiling in their company.

"Might wanna take that jacket and vest off, Bob," suggested Ken.

"Thanks, I think I will," I responded, while thinking to myself, "Might have helped to have done so a few minutes ago!"

Oh, well. Livin' and learnin'.

Just two weeks earlier I had moved, along with my wife and our infant daughter, from central Kansas to upstate New York—from a traditional wheat and cattle county, to a bedroom community that's home to state workers, educators, and professionals. We had lived in the Kansas setting for three years, during which I served a wonderful Presbyterian congregation. Though all too brief a stay, it nonetheless introduced me to the ebb and flow of an agrarian culture. I had fallen head over heals in love with it in no small measure because of the typically unreserved hospitality of the farming ethos.

However, there are always exceptions. One such had come in the form of an eighty year old priest who, I quickly learned, had recently been assigned to the Catholic parish in town by his bishop in Wichita. A few years before my family moved to the town, said bishop had reportedly become distressed by the progressive, ecumenical bent of the younger priest, who had been serving the parish for a handful of years. The bishop, betraying his conservative, pre-Vatican II upbringing, had decided to remove the younger, upstart priest. In his place the bishop then implanted into the parish his own contemporary, whose mission quite evidently was to bring the congregation back to the era when Catholics and Protestants didn't mesh or engage at all.

Beginning within my first two weeks in that Kansas town I experienced in person that regressive mission. On a regular basis the following played out. I would walk daily from my little church building to the town's post office to fetch the mail. I would frequently do so at the same time as the elderly priest, who would be coming from the other side of town. On each and every occasion, to my befuddlement, the priest would clearly spot me approaching him from the opposite direction, and then would cross the street in order to avoid meeting me face to face.

These recurrent episodes began to make me wonder, "Have I said something? Done something?" But we had never met, much less chatted. Somewhat hurt, but even more confused, I finally described this repetitive scenario to my newfound ministry friend, the Methodist pastor down the street. Upon hearing my consternation, he gently explained to me that the dear old priest had come into his pastoral vocation years back when Catholic priests avoided ecumenical engagement with Protestants of any and all ilk. His street-crossing routine was simply in keeping with his conscience. The Methodist pastor assured me that the priest, who knew exactly who I was from the large, front page picture of my wife and me in the newspaper that came out the day of our arrival, was simply doing what he felt was right.

So for the three years of Kansas life, I knew firsthand the experience of the odd, and even lonely, impact of institutional schism—of the brokenness of the wider church, and of the way it can mobilize behavior that maintains that very brokenness.

Then came our move to upstate New York in order to serve a special little Reformed congregation in a village that is also home to Lutheran and Catholic congregations. As I had been informed in no uncertain terms by my new congregation's pastoral search committee a few months earlier, there was one, non-negotiable obligation that I was expected to meet upon arrival. The committee chairperson had explained, "Each week you'll meet with the Lutheran minister and the Catholic priest. You'll do so in the

Catholic rectory, where these clergy meetings have been going on for years and years in our village."

I would be dishonest if I didn't confess to having some ambivalence on hearing that stipulation laid out so clearly. On the one hand, I have always been ecumenically inclined, valuing the opportunity to experience friendship and ministry with those from any and all expressions of the wider church. On the other hand, I had just completed three years of painful disconnect, and of disappointing and frustrating ostracism from any form of engagement with the priest in Kansas. While a part of me looked forward to the stipulated weekly meetings, another part of me was more than a bit unnerved by the unknowns.

Well, talk about being surprised.

The Tuesday arrived when I would have my first meeting with the Lutheran and Catholic pastors. Betraying my angst on rising that morning, I put on my best three piece suit—the same one I typically wore for, oh, funerals. Sweating a bit due to the late summer heat and humidity, not to mention my layered haberdashery, I pointedly knocked on the door of the rectory at precisely 10:00 a.m., as directed by my church administrative staff. "Hello," I called through the screen door. No answer. "Hello. Is this where the ministers' meeting is?" Still no answer. I carefully pushed open the door, tentatively entered, and proceeded to scout out the empty rectory. I found what appeared to be a lounge, complete with couch and armchairs. So I sat. I waited four minutes. Five minutes. Six minutes.

Just as I was ready to stand, breathe more easily, and take my leave, the screen door crashed open. In strode a jovial gent, slightly overweight, brush cut hair, and a huge smile on his face. Oh, and wearing only a grossly sweaty t-shirt, gym shorts, and running shoes, with one sock still high up on the calf, and the other flopping down by the ankle. "Looks like someone's been out jogging," I silently and brilliantly deduced. "In the muggy air, no less."

"You must be Bob!" he boomed. "I'm Ken. Welcome to town!"

With that, as I stood and moved toward him, this gentle Lutheran giant pushed aside my extended right hand, foregoing a handshake, and gave me the warmest, wettest hug I'd ever received. Just squeezed me to death. I swear I can still hear my heretofore clean vest protest.

Ken insisted that I sit back down. "Bob will be here any minute. The other Bob, of course." I nodded. "I just passed him on my run. He was going the opposite way, but he'll be circling back about now." Then, as was

Ken's wont, he boisterously declared his joy that this new, young pastor was finally here. "We've been looking forward to your arrival for a long time!"

Then before much else was exchanged, the screen door again flew open. In stumbled Bob, the Catholic priest, also finishing his morning jog. Also sweating like a dog. Or a Lutheran minister. Second verse, same as the first. Red in the face, perspiring like crazy, Bob walked right up to me. Just as I stood to greet him with a handshake, he too plowed right into me. Hugged me like we were the best of buddies. Tightly, with a warmth that still remains beyond description. "Boy, is it good to meet you, Bob!" the other Bob said to me. "Isn't it great, Ken?"

"Great! Just great!"

For obvious reasons it then hit me. "Well, I'm certainly not in Kansas anymore," I mumbled discretely to myself, while outwardly smiling in their company.

"Might wanna take that jacket and vest off, Bob," suggested Ken.

"Thanks, I think I will," I responded, while thinking to myself, "Might have helped to have done so a few minutes ago!"

With a welcome flourish, I pealed my jacket off, and then unbuttoned the vest, noting the newly imprinted smears. "Oh, well," I again thought to myself, "that's why they have cleaners." Stripped down to my shirt, I began to loosen, and then remove entirely, the carefully selected necktie that no longer needed to complement the suit.

That's when I noticed. Or more truthfully, that's when I gawked, at least for an instant before I gathered myself as if this were just any ordinary moment in my young ministry. There, hanging down from inside the right leg of Bob's soaked gym shorts, was a piece of cloth. Not some piece of holy cloth. It was the strap from his, uh, athletic supporter. I tried valiantly not to stare. But I failed. Bob, ever the quick observer, glanced down at his shorts. "Oh, look," he chuckled. "I missed the leg!" Ken erupted in laughter, as did Bob himself.

For a moment, I watched as the two of them chortled on about his having gotten only one leg into his jock strap. About how the priest had just run through the village with part of his supporter flapping in the wind for all to see. "Now that's something they'll be talking about for a while!" crowed Ken.

"Well, probably not," confessed a grinning Bob. "I doubt this is the first time I've ever done this." More whoops of laughter. I sat there, drinking it all in, feeling something heavenly about it all. I began to realize what a gift I had been given when instructed that I was to meet, every week, with these two amazing men.

Need I even say it? Over the years that followed, Ken and Bob became for me the unarguable models of what pastors are all about. What friendship looks like, and what it means to be vulnerable, joy-filled, living proof of the unity of God's one family.

12

Triangulated

THERE I SAT, THE only male in the large meeting room. More than three dozen women sat around me. Some stared at me in disbelief, others barely able to suppress open-mouthed smiles of pity. And then there were the three original complainants, all looking intently down at the song sheet in their laps. Last but not least there was dear Ethel, jaw jutting out, looking me in the eye with an unspoken challenge to say even one more word to her.

"This righteous battle is over, Bob," I thought to myself. "Time to shut up, retreat, and regroup."

Whence this moment of pastoral humbling? It started a month or so earlier. I was barely a handful of weeks into my new parish ministry in town, and within a span of ten days I had received three visits in my study. On each occasion a different woman had asked to speak with me privately about a concern she had regarding the women's guild in the parish.

For all practical purposes, I knew little about women's guilds, other than that my late mother attended and presided over the one in the congregation in which we were members during my junior and senior high school years. I had the vague idea that local guilds met for Bible study and service projects, as well as for mutual support and encouragement. So it was a bit disorienting when, during each of those three visits in my study, I listened to a female member of the congregation share her frustration about Ethel, the sixty-some year old treasurer of the congregation's women's guild. Each of the three described, presumably without coordination with the other two, her exasperation with Ethel. She had apparently served in her role as guild treasurer since, oh, forever, and ruled the guild's checkbook with uncompromising authoritarianism. All three women detailed to me how they had helped over the years with the guild's various fundraising efforts—rummage sales, ham suppers, and so forth—with the presumption that all the volunteers would have a say in how the raised monies would be used. However, each described how at the quarterly gatherings of the entire guild's membership, Ethel would report the net proceeds of the recent fundraisers, and then would announce how those proceeds would be used, be it for new pew cushions, or for an upgraded meat cutter, or what have you. But evidently Ethel made the call on her own, and did not countenance suggestions, much less objections, from the guild's wider membership.

Needless to say, by the time I had listened compassionately to the third complainant, my heart was stirred to action. If ever there were a local parish crusade that demanded attention, this situation was it. Though none of the three made any explicit request that I intervene with the guild, or with Ethel specifically, it was glaringly obvious that such an intervention was my holy duty and pastoral obligation.

Boy, was I ever suckered.

Now please understand, I was just three-plus years into ordained ministry. Back then in the mid-eighties, I was not yet introduced to the concept of being *triangulated*. I hadn't read about the pitfalls of being coaxed into meddling in a dust-up being experienced by two other individuals, including one (if not both) who manipulatively worked me into allying myself with them in their relational conflict. Well, my education about being triangulated was now underway, though I was blithely unaware of that fact.

Feeling a vocational responsibility to help the poor members of the women's guild find their voices in standing up to Ethel, I determined to be pastorally present for the next scheduled women's guild meeting. I contacted the elected president and offered to attend in order to "observe the workings of the guild and to learn what the guild was all about." The president gladly welcomed me to show up the following Monday night.

The evening arrived. My stomach was just a wee bit churning. I nonetheless walked into the gathering space, glad-handed several women, and found a seat on the far end of the second row. The president duly called the meeting to order. After a prayer and a general welcome, she pointed to me and welcomed me as a special guest, "here to learn about our guild." All the women graciously smiled in my direction, with a few saying aloud, "Nice to have you here, Pastor Bob."

The meeting then proceeded. A few business items were addressed, and before long Ethel, sitting beside the vice president and secretary at the head table, was invited to give the treasurer's report. Ethel strode to the podium. "Our checking account balance is a little more than $1,200," she began. "We raised $700 at the recent bake sale. We're sending our annual dues of $50 to the denomination's Office of Women's Work. That leaves enough to re-carpet the children's nursery, which has been in need of refurbishing for much too long. So we'll be installing new carpeting in that room. The total will be right around $800. Any questions?" She looked up at all of us seated before her. Not a word was spoken. Ethel then collected her notes and was about to walk back to her seat, when I heard my own voice.

"Ethel, I'm new here, trying to learn about the guild. I wonder if you'd be willing to explain how the decision about the carpeting was made. I'm always interested to learn how the church decides to do things."

"Well, everybody knows about the decisions." She stopped.

"How do you mean, Ethel?"

"Everybody knows when a decision has been made. Like right now. Everybody knows that we're buying carpeting for the nursery." She stared right at me. It was not an inviting stare. More like the one I remember my second grade teacher giving Sammy Parker when he said he had to go to the bathroom again, just seven minutes after returning from his first bathroom run.

"Is there a setting or process for that decision to be shared in, Ethel?"

"I just said. Everybody knows when a decision has been made." She again stopped. There I sat, the only male in the large meeting room. More than three dozen women sat around me. Some stared at me in disbelief, others barely able to suppress open-mouthed smiles of pity. And then there were the three original complainants, all looking intently down at the song sheet in their laps. Oh, and last but not least there was Ethel, jaw jutting out, looking me in the eye with an unspoken challenge to say even one more word to her.

"This righteous battle is over, Bob," I thought to myself. "Time to shut up, retreat, and regroup." But I could not leave well enough alone. I responded, "It sounds like you make the decision as the treasurer, and then inform everyone."

"If you say so," she said, with a little flint in her voice.

Time to shut up, retreat, and regroup. But no. "Well, I appreciate your clarifying that for me," I said, planning to say more. But before I could speak another word, Ethel responded.

"You're welcome." And then she headed back to her seat at the head table.

The president rushed up to the podium, and promptly announced, "We'll now hear from Gladys, who will describe our next fundraiser. Gladys?"

As Gladys regaled the assembly with an energetic and colorful explanation about the upcoming autumn tea festival, I sat in silence, trying to figure out what had just unfolded. I made no effort to conceal my looks directly at the three women who had spoken to me in my study. All three were glued to Gladys's every word. Not one of them looked in my direction. But several others did. Each looked at me with a smidge of maternal concern, not to mention an unabashed suggestion that I was a patsy—a well meaning patsy, but a patsy nonetheless. One even shook her head slightly while looking me in the eye, indicating that I had so, so much to learn in the years ahead.

My oh my, was she ever right.

13

Cloud of Witnesses

I'M NOT ONE WHO lightly calls a particular space "sacred." To the contrary, more often than not my instincts are to underscore the holy nature of *all* of creation. There is no place, no setting, where the divine is absent. Rather, our loving creator's presence abides in all who and in all that have been fashioned by that one's gracious imagination.

That being said, there's no question in my heart that certain particular spaces on unexpected occasions are transformed by a holy presence. They do become, even if fleetingly so, uniquely sacred.

Such is frequently the case during funeral and memorial services, when I have recommended over the years that the writer of the Letter to the Hebrews had it right. In the penultimate chapter of that formidable epistle, the letter writer conjures up the stirring image of our all being "surrounded by a great . . . cloud of witnesses." (Hebrews 12:1) It is to that image that I have regularly alluded during eulogistic remarks on the occasion of the life celebration of a recently deceased. I purposefully lift my right arm and circularly point above the heads of those in worship, sometimes in a sanctuary, sometimes in a funeral parlor, and sometimes graveside. While doing so I summon that wondrous phrase about the "great cloud of witnesses" who are surrounding us even here and now with a compassionate love and an unfathomable peace. I invite everyone in that sacred moment to see with faith-filled eyes that the recently departed is in fact not far, but near, in that invisible but present cloud of living souls giving witness to the reality of life beyond this life. Giving witness to the love that promises to weep with, and ultimately to heal, the departed's grieving survivors.

In those instances the otherwise ordinary space—the sanctuary, the parlor, the graveside—becomes sacred. Not because it is of itself sacred, but because of that cloud, that witnessing presence.

But then there was that day early in my years of ministry when one of that cloud's witnesses was indisputably present. She was, in fact, visible and aural.

Abby was dying. A beloved member of the congregation, an extraordinary daughter, sister, wife, and mother, Abby was physically ravaged by cancer, barely in her forties. Receiving hospice care at home, she had decided to forego any further intervention other than to receive heavy pain medication.

For the better part of a week she was essentially comatose. I had stopped by at noontime, as I had daily for two straight weeks, in order to have quiet prayer with her, albeit presuming her likely inability to hear what was being intoned on her behalf. I had returned to the church and secluded myself for some preliminary preparation for her impending funeral. Then mid-afternoon, while sadly listing biblical texts and pastoral memories on my legal pad, the phone rang. It was Abby's husband. Rod said quietly, "Would you please come back to the house, Bob? We've decided to get the whole family around Abby, and we want you and Ken to have some prayer with her and us together."

My Lutheran counterpart and spiritual mentor, Ken met me at the front door of their home within the hour. We walked in to a heart-rending sight. Gathered in a circle of some twenty in number were three generations of the family, with Abby, bless her heart, embedded in her recliner in their midst. She was as I had seen her just hours earlier, cocooned in supporting pillows, head severely drooping forward in apparent sleep, eyes closed, breathing only intermittently.

Ken and I embraced everyone and then sat as part of their circle. On Rod's request, Ken and I both prayerfully asked for God's gracious presence. Our prayers were simple, tearfully heartfelt.

Then Ken, wizened pastor that he was, invited everyone in the circle to say a word or two to Abby. It was an extraordinary invitation. And it was welcomed. One after another, Abby's loved ones spoke. "You're a wonderful daughter, Abby." "We love you so much, Mom." "What times we've had since our wedding day, love."

It was sacred.

And then Abby whispered. As a witness from the cloud, but right there with us. "Ah lah yeh teh."

I love you, too.

There were gasps, with not another word spoken. Tears streamed, mouths fell agape, and everyone leaned forward.

That was all. And that was everything.

Sacred.

There we all were, surrounded by the cloud now made visible and aural in the person of Abby. By the witness in our midst who spoke, not only her own love for her family, but the love of the one who had given her to each of us as daughter, wife, mother, and sister in Christ.

Abby passed away within the hour, and in doing so she became even more a part of the great cloud of witnesses who still encircle each of us daily, wherever we may be, not just in churches or parlors or cemeteries, but everywhere.

Listen for their witness. It whispers of eternal love, enfleshed not just two millennia ago, but sacredly in our midst every moment of every day.

14

Voice for Justice

"PLEASE UNDERSTAND, NORMAN. I believe her, not you."

The look in his eyes was one of shock and disappointment. "Oh," Norman said. "Oh."

I had been dreading that very moment for several days, or maybe for several years. Almost four decades my senior, Norman was what is oftentimes labeled a pillar of the church: a long time member, now professionally retired, but still very active within the congregation's life. A member of the adult choir for years and years along with Ethel, his beloved wife of well more than half a century, Norman had served on most all of the committees of the church. In fact, he had been a member of the governing board at the time of my installation as the new pastor when I was thirty-one.

Norman and I had become good friends, at least to the extent that the pastor-parishioner relationship permits. He and Ethel regularly welcomed me for informal pastoral visits and had always made me feel at home.

However it wasn't more than a year into my ministry that I began to hear comments. They were not accusations, but were thinly veiled asides from women in the congregation. In each and every instance the women suggested Norman intruded uncomfortably into their space. When I would ask for clarification, the description included uninvited hugs that were reported to be both overly physical and unnecessarily long. I observed Norman over a period of time, and though I did not witness behavior that was unarguably blatant, it nonetheless tended to corroborate the women's complaints.

In retrospect, I confess to being far too slow to intervene, far too slow to confront.

All of that changed when I received the phone call that forced the issue. Bernadette left a message on my voice mail, requesting in a firm tone that she needed to talk with me. I reached her the same day, and we scheduled a visit for the following morning.

It wasn't more than five seconds after Bernadette and I had taken our seats in my study, having exchanged warm greetings as she had walked in, when she declared, "Bob, you have to do something, and it has to be right away."

"How so, Bernadette? What's up?"

"It's Norman," she began. "He has to be stopped, or else I'm going to the police." Over the course of the next hour Bernadette gut-wrenchingly described how she had for years been inappropriately hugged by Norman wherever they met, be it in the sanctuary on Sundays or at the post office, gas station, or wherever on weekdays. She reported how she had repeatedly asked him not to give her hugs. Hand shakes were welcome, but nothing more. Yet he had persisted. All the while, noted Bernadette, she watched as any number of other women in the congregation, not to mention in the wider village, had been enduring comparable harassment by Norman. "But no more, Bob. No more. I refuse to let this go on, maybe even end up having my daughters become victims. I'm prepared to bring charges, and I've already talked informally with the police about doing so."

I sat there, listening and realizing I believed her. Every word. I had no doubt she would indeed do whatever it took to bring Norman's behavior to a stop. Now. And for good.

Which led inexorably to the meeting in my study, just a handful of days later. On my invitation Norman came to the study, knowing only that it was for the purpose of conversation with Bernadette and me. Once we had all taken our seats, I said, "Norman, Bernadette came to me very recently in order to discuss you and your behavior. I've invited her to speak with you, while I'm present, so the two of you can consider together what she's very concerned about."

Norman nodded, looking at me and then at Bernadette. He shuffled his feet on the carpet, understandably now ill at ease. "What is it, Bernadette?"

Then, to my undiluted amazement, she spoke directly. Sometimes tearfully, but even more so, angrily. "Norman, you have for too long sexually harassed me, not to mention other women in the church as well. It's going to stop. Today. And if it doesn't, I'm going to bring you up on charges, and I'll let the police do whatever it takes to make you stop." She caught her breath. She collected herself for a moment, while Norman sat there, staring first at her and then at the floor. Then she said, "And Norman, you will never, ever touch my daughters. It stops now."

I sat there, silent, looking first at Bernadette, then at Norman. It's hard to recall how long the silence lasted. It may have been two seconds, maybe twenty-two. But then Norman responded. "Bernadette, I think you're mistaken. I've never hugged, or touched, or anything in a wrong way."

Bitterly she said, "You have. Again and again, even after I've asked you to stop."

Silence.

Norman finally spoke. "Bob, I really don't know what she's talking about. I would never do such things."

Then, because I knew I had to speak for the voices that had been either ignored or silenced, I said, "Please understand, Norman. I believe her, not you."

The look in his eyes was one of shock and disappointment. "Oh," Norman said. "Oh."

Thirty minutes later Norman excused himself, having pledged with as sad a tone in his voice as I've ever heard, that he would not touch Bernadette or her daughters, and that he would not be inappropriate with any women. Bernadette had responded by saying she would be watching—as did I.

Upon Bernadette's departure a few minutes after Norman's, I sat stock-still in my chair. It felt as though I had passed through a tunnel of some sort, or a valley that needed to be traversed in order to get where I was called to be. I was drained. Sad, but stronger.

The following Monday, after seeing neither Norman nor Ethel in worship that Sunday morning, I phoned their home and asked if I might stop by for a short visit at their convenience. Ethel, who had answered, said, "Of course. We'd love to have you."

I drove over to their home, steeling myself for—what? I couldn't fathom what awaited me when I walked into their home. I had never, in my first few years in ministry, been in just such a circumstance.

Norman answered the doorbell, opened the door, and ushered me into their warm living room. There sat his beloved Ethel, knitting. She rose and gave me a gentle hug, inviting me to sit in my customary chair. "Thank you for allowing me to come over, friends," I began. "I wanted to see how you are."

I had no idea whether Norman had shared one iota about the confrontation in my study the previous week. At one level I anticipated the real possibility Ethel was sitting there, totally in the dark. Side by side on the couch, they looked at each other, then simultaneously at me. It was dear Ethel who spoke first. "Bob, I understand Bernadette doesn't want my husband to hug her, or to touch her daughters. Norman told me about everything." She stopped. I nodded, looking at both of them. Sensing Ethel had more to say, I remained silent. Then, referring to two members of the church who were about the same age as Norman and Ethel, she continued. "What I don't get, Bob, is that both Sam and Carlton did that kind of stuff to me and to all my women friends in the church from back when we were all teenagers. But nobody ever told them to stop doing it. We just had to live with it. And we did. Even Norman knew we did. So I don't get why Norman is being singled out of all the men that do this stuff to all of us women."

I sat without moving. How does one respond to something that was the farthest thing that one could ever have imagined hearing? I was truly dumbstruck.

Ethel looked me in the eye, seemingly waiting for a response, or not. Maybe it wasn't a response she was awaiting. Maybe it was simply a moment when an injustice was being declared, an injustice that had gone on, unchallenged, for well more than half a century.

Whether she was expecting a response or not, I spoke. "Ethel, I'm deeply sorry you and so many others like you have had to endure that kind of injury and harassment, with no one standing up for you. We in the church have let you down. It's going to stop now. I pledge to you to do what I can to make it so."

She nodded, patted her husband on the knee, and said, "Thank you, Bob."

The visit continued, with a bit more focus on how we could all share in safeguarding the wellbeing and dignity of girls and women, as well as others in the church and village who may experience victimization of any sort.

Within a year the church's governing board had drafted and affirmed a congregation-wide policy on appropriate physical contact. Guess who shared in that work, and who returned to be part of the congregation? And guess whose funerals I had over the course of the following decade?

I miss Norman and Ethel dearly.

But, in the same vein, I am profoundly grateful that Bernadette, along with her adolescent daughters, also remained a part of the congregation, modeling for me what it means to be strong. What it means to be a living voice for justice.

15

Holy

THERE ARE MOMENTS IN one's pastoral pilgrimage that veer away from the ordinary, the mundane. They cry out, after the fact, to be called "holy." And rarely, if ever, does the pastor see them coming.

That was again and again the case in my own pilgrimage, but none more so than on that otherwise ordinary afternoon in my study when I received a call from the intensive care unit in a nearby hospital. The message was simple, and though not frequently received, it was not unique. The charge nurse, after she and I clarified who each of us was, said I had best get to the hospital immediately. One of my parishioners, who had given her my name, was dying. At the sadly young age of forty-nine, Trevor had asked that his pastor come be with him at the very end of his earthly life.

I shut down whatever was demanding my attention and drove to the hospital "with haste," ironically not unlike young Mary, off to Elizabeth's home after Gabriel's shocking announcement to her. (See Luke 1:39) While driving I inevitably found my thoughts drifting back to the various conversations I had had over the past few years with Trevor. None of them had ever been brusque or shallow. No, Trevor was a man of quiet substance and of generous spirit. He had battled diabetes since his teens and had found it a daily grind to manage the disease. He had told me on a couple of occasions, with a quiet smile on his face, he did not expect to live to see fifty. Recalling those conversations I began to tear up over his foresight.

Oh, Trevor. Not yet fifty.

After parking I moved quickly into the hospital, down the long hallway, up the elevator, down the shorter hallway, and through the ICU doors. The charge nurse, figuring out immediately who I was, pointed toward the curtained off cubicle at the far end of many. White coated staff were wandering in and out of several of the cubicles, but none in and out of Trevor's as I approached. I pulled aside the curtain, finding myself standing at the end of his bed. His eyes were closed, but his face was astonishingly at peace. For a moment I thought myself too late.

But then he opened his right eye, looked at me standing over his toes, and smiled gently. "*Domine*," he said, echoing what he had ritually called me for the duration of our friendship. *Domine*, just as old Dutch ministers had been called in a distant era, and which his late and beloved mother had trained him as a boy was the right title for one's pastor.

I moved to his side and took his right hand in mine. We simply looked each other in the eye. I was already teary, but could see through the resulting mistiness that he was not. His face, if it's possible to say it, was clear, fresh, at peace. It was ready.

We talked quietly for a few minutes, his explaining as best he could what had led to his ambulance ride and subsequent conversation with his doctor here in the ICU. How the two of them had agreed that Trevor was dying, and how Trevor wanted no measures to be taken, with one exception. Call his minister, his *domine*.

Then the holy happened. He told me what he admitted he hadn't told anyone in twenty-eight years. He told me that when he was twenty-one he had died on a hospital transport cart, probably due to diabetic vulnerabilities. During that time, what we so easily label a near-death experience, he had moved through a tunnel of light and had seen God.

God.

He told me he had felt loved and embraced, and that he didn't want to "come back here." "But," he went on, "God said, 'Not yet, Trevor. You have a mother to care for. In time, though, you'll return.'" He then said to me, with unquenchable peacefulness, "I came back. Here." To that very hospital, he made it clear. He told me he had awakened, somewhat morose that he was back. Determined, he recovered and then cared for his beloved mother until her passing.

He then described how, the day following his having seen God, he told a pastor who came to see him in the hospital whom it was he had seen while lying unresponsive the previous day. The pastor responded, explained Trevor, by saying patronizingly, "Well, lots of people hallucinate when they're gravely ill, don't they." It wasn't a question. It was a statement.

Trevor then told me that from that moment on, for twenty-eight years he had decided he would tell no one about his having seen God. Pearls before swine, and such.

I was struck dumb in that moment. I squeezed Trevor's right hand, tears streaming over my quivering lips. Then Trevor told me this. He told me he was at peace. He was ready. He was not afraid in the least. He was going home, and he couldn't wait.

Holy.

Shortly thereafter Trevor indeed went home, again to be with his God, to be embraced, and to be loved.

I still tear up at the gift that Trevor was, and that Trevor gave.

Holy.

16

Honesty

I WAS SO SHOCKED—AND enraged—I gave consideration to getting up and walking out. Though I didn't, I've thought on occasion doing so might well have been the right thing to do.

I was a delegate to a meeting of a regional assembly of my denomination. Typically this meeting entailed reports given and decisions made by the several dozen delegates assigned to attend. This occasion's meeting was exceptional, however. Where normally the first of its meeting days would be given to committee presentations and the like, this year's first day was spent in "judicial session." That is, we delegates were all participants in the regional assembly's version of a trial.

A pastor was on trial. Charges had been levied against him in the wake of his having officiated the previous year at the wedding of his son and his son's now husband. Given some delegates' strong views about homosexuality, those delegates had predictably taken issue with the pastor's actions, and were demanding that the assembly hold him ecclesiastically accountable.

To no one's surprise, the trial unfolded with tension and bitterness. By the end of the excruciating, day-long process, a majority of the delegates—with all of us serving as the jury—voted to find him culpable. The ensuing sentence included the pastor's suspension from his ordained office. That is, he was prohibited from preaching, celebrating the sacraments, and so forth, until and unless he would confess his misdeeds. This, he openly stated, he would not do, given his conviction that he had not done anything wrong in God's eyes.

The aftermath of the trial was not just one of apparent satisfaction for those who had brought the charges, but one of deep sadness and frustration for many of us who had objected to those charges in the first place. Inevitably I slept only fitfully that night.

Then day two of the regional assembly arrived, and we delegates returned for the more typical agenda concerns of the meeting. All several dozen of us sat fairly quietly and tensely through report after report, occasionally being asked to vote on one or another proposal. It was when one such vote was being taken the shocking moment unfolded.

Tellers had been sent into a side room in order to hand count the paper ballots on which the delegates had marked our votes on one or another question. The presiding chair of the assembly—a genial and capable pastor who had been elected to the one year position during the previous year's comparable meeting—then took it upon himself to "fill the gap," he explained. While all the delegates sat in relative silence, waiting for the tellers to return and report the results of the ballot count, the presiding chair announced, "My predecessor told me I should be sure to come prepared to fill these occasional times when work is held up by the tellers' counts. He said, 'Be sure to bring some jokes to fill the time.' So, I hunted up some church jokes."

As the presiding chair then fumbled a bit through his briefcase for those jokes, we delegates sat silently, not sure what to expect. In short order he found the sought-after paper and set it on the lectern. Ready to begin reading, he declared, "These are titles of hymns that could possibly be used in other situations than worship. For example, what might be a good hymn for a bride to sing to her new husband on their wedding night?" Silence. He then answered his own question, saying, "How about 'Come, Thou Fount of Every Blessing'?"

For a moment there was no response from the gathered delegates. Then, an eruption of laughter from at least half a dozen individuals—all male—loudly guffawing at the raw, sexual innuendo embedded in the punch line. The presiding officer nodded his appreciation toward the handful of men who had responded with laughs.

Meanwhile, I sat in my seat, stunned beyond words. And I was not alone. I glanced all around me. The vast majority of faces, both female and male, were staring at the presiding chair up on the dais. Most all of our mouths were open in shock. In dismay. In disbelief.

Prompted by the six or more laughers, the presiding chair continued, sharing one or two more jokes that were undisguised in their lurid, sexual inferences.

No one moved, including me. But I was so shocked—and enraged— I gave consideration to getting up and walking out. Though I didn't, I've thought on occasion doing so might well have been the right thing to do.

Within a minute or two, the tellers returned from their room and handed to the presiding chair the vote tally. He announced the results and then calmly returned the sheet of paper with the "hymn-jokes" to his brief-case. He called us back to our order of business, with not a word more said about those abhorrent jokes.

The balance of the day was a blur to me—not because of the pace of the assembly's work, but because of the residue of confusion and disgust I continued to feel in the aftermath of hearing those jokes. For the life of me, I could not fathom how the presiding chair could so blatantly engage in such crude behavior—especially in light of what we had just been through the day before. "How could he," I wondered to myself, "make sexual jokes—out of Christian hymns, no less—only hours after presiding over a trial where sexuality was the serious focus?" Most confounding was that it had been somewhat apparent during the trial the presiding chair was in agreement that the charged pastor was in the wrong for having definitively affirmed same-gender relationships. If homosexuality was an issue of such repug-nance to the presiding chair, how could he now so easily, even breezily, tell blatantly "dirty jokes" to the same assembly?

That evening, after the meeting's adjournment, I stewed. I mulled.

Until a picture began to take shape. A possible explanation began to come into focus.

I found myself reviewing two factors that had been at play. First, the joke-telling presiding chair was male, and he had alluded from the dais to his being married and father to several wonderful children. That is, he was making clear he was straight—most definitely *not* homosexual. Second, he was a pastor, who likely saw fit to preach—maybe at least annually?—about the sanctity of heterosexual marriage. If he indeed had biblical objection to homosexuality, it would be understandable he would feel a vocational obligation to lift up the biblical insistence on chaste heterosexuality. Presumably his congregation would concur and expect, even demand, his doing so.

"But," I found myself musing, "what if that same pastor, for any number of reasons, might never have had or made the opportunity, in a safe setting—say, with a skilled therapist—to examine sexuality as a whole, much less his own? What if he was indeed straight, married, monogamous, and vocationally committed to the virtues of faithful heterosexual marriage, but had never explored instances—inclinations?—that might have entailed any fleeting departure from those virtues? And maybe just as significantly, what if he was—unconsciously?—somewhat uncomfortable with human sexuality, including his own, *overall*? Or what if he was afraid that some unexamined instances when he had found himself thinking unchaste thoughts, even as a heterosexual individual, might somehow come to light—might be discovered by his loved ones, his peers, or his parishioners? It would be understandable that he would make every effort to avoid such potentially embarrassing, even vocationally endangering, revelations coming to light."

Mulling over the above, it hit me. How best to avoid any such possibility of "being discovered?" Do two things: first, point to others whose sexuality is easily assailable, especially by one's cohorts and friends; and second—and ironically—make light of sexuality, suggesting that one has one's own sexuality in healthy condition.

The first of those two things makes sense. If one can point to a bogeyman—say, someone who is homosexual, and therefore easily assailed—then everyone will look at the bogeyman rather than at the heterosexual one doing the pointing.

The second of those two things makes less sense. And yet it *does* make odd sense. Making light of sexuality—say, by telling "dirty jokes"—conveys to the hearers that the teller of the objectionable jokes is comfortable with sexuality, including one's own. Why else do male athletes engage in the odd custom of "locker room humor" about sexuality, other than to prove to one another—even to themselves—that each has a handle on his own (hetero) sexuality?

It hit me. There on the floor of our regional assembly meeting, it was *possible* that a straight male pastor had—unconsciously?—engaged in the sordid business of "locker room humor" in order to ensure that everyone—including himself—knew that he was healthy, even if others, including those who are gay and those who "support" those who are gay, were not.

Maybe his telling "dirty jokes," using Christian hymns, became a way to prove that he, compared to "those gays," had his own sexual house in biblical order.

Needless to say, my conjecture that night was purely that—conjecture. Yet it somehow helped me to make potential sense of an otherwise absurd and distressing experience.

Am I convinced my conjecture veered close to the truth? No. But I suspect that it *might* have. If so, that conjecture helps me to make some sense of the apparently nonsensical and reprehensible. And it potentially speaks to the need for each and all of us in the church—*especially* those of us who are straight males in pulpits—to be fully self-aware and honest with ourselves about human sexuality. Absent such honesty, we may fall victim, all too easily, to being assaultive of others.

17

Whoops

BEN, MY PEER IN ministry, was already beginning to chuckle, somehow anticipating what Ken was going to say. When Ken actually said it, I joined in, bursting out laughing, sitting forward in my chair almost in disbelief. "You're *kidding*, Ken!"

"Nope. I wish I were." At which point he, too, started laughing right along with Ben and me.

The three of us had just sat down for our Tuesday morning, weekly clergy gabfest. Before we had fully settled into our easy chairs, Ken, my Lutheran friend and pastoral mentor, declared somewhat soberly to Ben and me, "Well, yesterday I did what I never knew I would—or could—do."

"What was that?" I asked, just a bit nervous about what this model minister in my life was going to confess.

"Well, I went to see Winnie Thompson's elderly, widowed aunt yesterday." I knew Winnie to be one of Ken's dearest parishioners. "I first met Mrs. Hunter, the aunt, last week when she was admitted to the Good Samaritan nursing facility in Schenectady. Winnie asked me to call on her aunt, since she didn't have a church home, and could use a little pastoral care." Ben and I nodded, listening intently as Ken proceeded with a serious expression on his face. "I visited her a couple times last week, and then dropped in to see her again yesterday. I walked into her room, and could tell she wasn't doing very well. As I took my coat off, she didn't respond to my voice when I let her know I was here to see her again on her niece's behalf." Ken stopped for a moment, took a gulp from his hot coffee mug, and then said somewhat dramatically, "I pulled a chair up next to her bed, sat down, and then stayed for fifteen minutes of quiet prayer. She wasn't waking up for me, but I wasn't surprised, since she had been pretty out of it when I was with her last Friday. I recited the twenty-third Psalm, and then informed her I was going to have a prayer with her before heading on my way."

Ben and I continued to listen quietly, nodding in empathetic support. Each of us could well have said aloud, "Been there, done that."

Ken continued. "When I finished my prayer, I bent over her and gave her a light kiss on the forehead. I then picked up my coat, and was pulling it on when a nurse walked in behind me." Ben and I nodded. "She stepped quietly past me and asked, 'Are you family, sir?' I said, 'No, I'm her niece's pastor.' She then said, 'Well, my condolences to the whole family.' And then she stepped up to the side of the bed, and pulled the sheet straight up and over the woman's head!"

Ken stopped. Ben was already beginning to chuckle, somehow anticipating what Ken was going to say. When Ken actually said it, I joined in, burst out laughing, sitting forward in my chair, almost in disbelief. "You're *kidding*, Ken!"

"Nope. I wish I were." At which point he, too, started laughing right along with Ben and me. "I didn't dare say anything to that nurse," he continued. "But I wanted to sort things out, so I went out to the nurses' station and solemnly asked the clerk, 'Excuse me, but how long ago did Mrs. Hunter pass away?' She told me, 'Oh, maybe forty-five minutes ago. We reached her niece, and she just called back to say that the funeral home folks will be along any minute.'" Ben and I were howling at this point. Ken continued, his ample belly shaking. "I told her thanks in as serious a voice as possible, and then I got the hell out of there before anyone could figure out what I'd just done!"

The laughter in our room was loud enough to be heard throughout the whole village, had the windows been open. The subsequent storytelling around our circle of three turned both professionally confessional and personally supportive, just as our weekly conversations inevitably were.

From that morning on I found myself ever so careful each time I wandered into a nursing home or hospital room and found the person I was there to visit appearing to be asleep. I became, as one might guess, adept at assessing that person's condition. No way was I ever going to shuffle into any future Tuesday clergy gathering and end up having to reprise my beloved friend's confessional.

18

Parental Love

NAOMI HAD DESCRIBED JAY to me earlier. Described, truth be told, in quite some detail during the pre-marriage pastoral counseling sessions I had had during the twelve months leading up to Naomi and Neville's wedding. Naomi had explained to me that her biological father, Jay, had left her mother when Naomi was an infant. For the past two decades and more, Jay had visited Naomi on just a handful of occasions, typically without warning ahead of time.

According to Naomi, Jay was an alcoholic, with a messy history of multiple jobs and broken homes. During those brief visits he and Naomi had had, she described him as uncomfortably self-absorbed, with little interest in her life story. She had endured their conversations, but had always felt relieved when he had grabbed his jacket, given her a peck on a cheek, and departed, not to be seen or heard from again for long periods of time, typically two or more years.

Naomi had also described for me how her mother had raised her on her own until remarrying when Naomi was in kindergarten. Hubert became Naomi's new father, providing her with wonderful paternal affection and trustworthy familial stability. If and when Hubert happened to be around when Jay would come to visit Naomi, Hubert made a point of being close at hand, "just in case," explained Naomi.

As Naomi and Neville's wedding date drew closer, the three of us began to map out the details surrounding the impending rehearsal and wedding service. To her credit, before I even asked her about it, Naomi quietly suggested we needed to give strategic consideration ahead of time to the outside possibility that Jay would show up at one or both of those settings. When I asked, Naomi shook her head vehemently, saying, "No, I most certainly am not planning on inviting him, Pastor Bob." Sadly looking down at the floor of my study and then back up at me, she said, "But there's always a possibility he'll find out about our wedding." When she said that, she visibly shuddered, wrapping her arms around herself.

So we planned. We brainstormed various scenarios. We did so in such detail one would have thought we would be prepared for virtually anything come the weekend of the wedding.

But it's one thing to plan. It's another to deal with the actual moment.

The wedding weekend arrived. It was late afternoon on Friday, and some twenty of us were gathered in the sanctuary for the rehearsal. I was standing front and center, with the entire wedding party semi-circling me. Naomi, her left arm securely hooked into the paternal right arm of step-father Hubert, was planted directly opposite me, with her fiancé Neville quietly, proudly standing to her immediate right. Several attendants stood to the right and left of the threesome. We were some twenty minutes into the walk-through portion of the rehearsal, when all of a sudden the side entryway door into the sanctuary burst open and in walked a man I'd never seen before. "Hey!" he cried. "Couldn't wait for the father of the bride?"

All heads immediately swiveled in his direction. Jaws dropped. There were several gasps of disbelief, if not horror. There stood Jay. Or more accurately, there wobbled Jay, even before he began walking toward the wedding party. I quickly glanced at Naomi, whose eyes betrayed a sense of disbelief. Her shoulders visibly sagged.

Although Naomi, Neville, and I had battle-planned for just this kind of moment, the reality was still stunning and briefly immobilizing. For an instant I stood there, watching Jay as he began to semi-weave his way from the side door toward the wedding party. Then, as if on cue, the wedding party scattered. The bridal attendants jumped away from the advancing menace. Neville swiftly stepped forward, right in front of both his bride and Hubert. The best man and the three other groomsmen bolted from what had just been the bridal semi-circle, grabbing Neville by his arms, restraining him from moving into the breach. While two of them held him back, the other two moved directly in front of Jay, legs parted, walling off Jay from approaching any closer to Neville or Naomi.

To my dismay, Jay pulled his right arm back in a gesture foreshadowing a roundhouse swing at the twosome now standing in his way. Just as he began to let his punch fly, the two young men grabbed his arms, pinned them to his side, and growled, "Not here, sir. Not now. Not ever."

That's when I found my tongue. "Jay, is it?" I asked the invader.

He nodded. "That's me," he managed. "I'm here to walk my daughter down the aisle. That's my right, and nobody's gonna take that right away from me." He looked agitatedly from me to Naomi, and then at Hubert, who was now holding Naomi securely with his arms encircling her with undisguised, protective determination.

I walked up to Jay and was immediately bowled over by the smell of alcohol. "No, you're not going to do that, Jay. Naomi has rightly asked Hubert to do so. And Naomi and Neville have understandably chosen not to have you present, either tonight or tomorrow afternoon." Jay stared angrily at me. More calmly than I would ever have guessed I could be, I declared, "You'll leave right now, Jay. Now."

With that, the two groomsmen promptly lifted Jay off his feet and carried him out the same door he had used just a minute earlier.

By now Naomi was in tears, as was her mother, sitting in shock in the first pew. I asked the entire wedding party to be seated, with the exception of the groomsmen, whom I assigned guard duty at the various entryways into the sanctuary. I then ushered Naomi, Neville, Hubert, and Naomi's mother to my study, where for a few minutes tears were shed, shock was confessed, and plans were strategized for the next twenty-four hours. To her lasting credit, Naomi managed to recapture a small smile, albeit with eyes red and hands still shaking. Only when she declared herself ready to return to the sanctuary, the five of us headed back. In what seemed like a scene out of some unbelievable fiction, I then tried to coach the entire wedding party, along with a smattering of additional family members, how we were going to proceed, both with the rehearsal, as well as with the wedding the next day. It's fair to say the careful attentiveness of that entire assembly far surpassed that of any other of my wedding rehearsals, either before or since.

Come Saturday afternoon, a small army of suited, brawl-ready friends of the bride and groom stood at all the doors into the sanctuary, with a couple even on station outside, eyeing the parking lot and street with the unabashed demeanor of a Mafia boss's henchmen. Inside the sanctuary the wedding unfolded with nary a surprise. I watched with awe from the head of the aisle as Naomi, glowing with affection for Neville, who stood beside me, walked down that aisle on Hubert's protective arm. The two of them were a marvel to behold, embodying to perfection what a father and daughter are all about. Not just at a wedding, but always.

19

The Right Decision

"Grab a bat, Joe. You're on deck." Hearing those words, I instantly turned from watching the pitcher to staring in disbelief at Mark.

Joe, as equally shocked as I and everyone else on the home team bench, stammered in response to Mark, "You sure?"

"Absolutely. You'll be batting in my place," declared Mark, almost as if it were the most obvious managerial move to make under the circumstances.

But the circumstances made no such case. To bat Joe in Mark's place was absurd. Everyone on our bench knew it. Yet, absurd as it was, it bordered on the divine. Or more to the point, it bordered on the human.

A little background. Mark and Joe and the rest of us comprised our church's undefeated softball team. We had made it unscathed through the whole spring season of competition with the other church teams in our division, in no small measure because of Mark, our captain, who incidentally had played in the New York Yankees minor leagues during his twenties. We most certainly were not undefeated because of Joe, who would be the first to chuckle and admit it. Not once ever able to bat the ball out of the infield all season long—when he even put bat on ball—Joe was the last man on our team's bench. He delighted in cheering on all of us, his teammates, and would typically be subbed in during the last inning or two, once the run differential had hit double digits and our right fielder was ready to rest his chronically sore back.

We had made it all the way to the championship game, now facing down the undefeated squad from the church league's other division of teams. Two ecclesiastical powerhouses, comprised mostly of wannabe athletes in our thirties and forties. Most of us had played ball in younger years, but with one at significantly higher levels than the rest. Not many congregations can boast a former Yankees minor leaguer batting third in the order.

This final game of the season had played itself out with competitive tension. After six innings it was tied, two all. Then the drama of the seventh and decisive inning.

Our rivals managed to push across a run in the top of the inning, then took the field. Our team's collection of thirteen guys gathered around the home team bench, grunting encouragement, urging one another on to a rally and a dreamed about, undefeated championship season. The first batter hit the ball on the line, but right at their left fielder. One out, only two outs left. But we all knew: Mark was scheduled to bat third, and he always had the capacity to drive the ball well over any right fielder's head, given his sweet lefty's swing. Our team's second batter strode to the plate, with cheers from our bench. He settled into the hitter's box, taking a couple of practice swings. And then Mark called out, "Grab a bat, Joe. You're on deck."

"You sure?"

"Absolutely. You'll be batting in my place."

Joe, more than a bit hesitantly, stood up and took hold of a bat. He stared at it as if for the first time. Mark, the object of a bench full of slack-jawed gawks, clapped his hands and cheered on the inning's second batter, who promptly popped out to shortstop. Two outs. Only one more out left in the game. In the season. In our hopes for an undefeated championship. Then Mark cheerfully cried out, "Go get 'em, Joe!" Others of us echoed Mark's urging, but admittedly with less zeal.

Joe stepped timidly into the batter's box. He awkwardly took a practice swing, immediately revealing to the team in the field that he knew very little about how to bat. With some caution, all the fielders crept toward the plate. And rightly so. The first pitch looped toward home plate, and Joe flailed awkwardly at the ball, almost tipping over in the process. But he hit it. Barely. The ball dribbled back to the pitcher, who whipped the ball to the first baseman before Joe had barely righted himself in the batter's box, much less begun to trundle his way down the base path. "Out!" called the ump near first base. A wild cheer erupted from the opposing team—the undefeated, championship winning team.

For a few seconds, only silence from our home team bench, including me. Until we all heard Mark call out, "Way to swing the bat, Joe!" He did so with as warm a smile on his face as one could ever imagine.

Absurd. But bordering on the divine, even on the human.

Then something even more unscriptable happened. After the victorious team in the field had high-fived each other with whoops of joy, they all started looking right at Mark, with stares of confusion and expressions of respect.

They knew. We all knew. Mark had made the right decision.

Did anyone lose that evening? Wrong question.

Fast forward two decades. I'm standing in the pulpit, eyes welling up. To my left and just below stands a casket, surrounded by dozens of floral arrangements. Mark's fifty-nine year old widow and two grown children sit in close proximity, surrounded by well more than seven hundred worshipers. The day before, more than twenty-three hundred had stood in line at the funeral home, waiting patiently to pay their respects to this loved one and friend who had succumbed to cancer at much too young an age. The funeral director had mentioned quietly to Mark's family that more had come to Mark's viewing than had come to that of the late mayor of Albany, capital city of New York state.

I don't know whether in attendance at the memorial service were any members of the team that had scored three runs that evening twenty years earlier. I suspect there were. But what I do know is virtually every one of Mark's teammates, who together had managed to push across only two runs that same evening, *were* present. Including Joe.

20

Never, Ever

"Okay, Pastor Bob. You asked? Then I'll tell you." And Janelle did. Although that was well more than two decades ago, I still recall it with sobering clarity.

Some six months earlier I had sat in the overly crowded sanctuary of the neighboring Roman Catholic parish. My ten year old daughter pressed up against my side as we watched in silent distress, along with several hundred others. Janelle, her husband, and their surviving daughter and son, walked behind the casket. Midway down the aisle Janelle began to wail uncontrollably, tugging on her red-eyed husband's arm as if to implore, "No. I. Can. *Not.* Do. This."

Five days had passed since their ten year old daughter had succumbed to a shockingly quick and deadly sepsis—healthy one day, gone less than forty-eight hours later. I didn't personally know the family. But our daughter Emily had come to know from school the young girl whose passing we were now mourning. Indicating to my wife and me that she wanted to attend the funeral, I had agreed to accompany Emily.

The weeks and months then passed. I heard informal bits and pieces about Janelle and her grieving family from their priest, as well as from members of my own congregation. Understandably, reports suggested that both parents were profoundly despondent, but were necessarily pressing on with life, including caring for their surviving son and daughter.

Then the call came. "Bob, I've told Janelle about you. I've suggested that she and you might have a chat sometime." Brigitte, a member of my congregation, continued. "Janelle and I see each other regularly. I'm concerned about her. She's both bereaved and angry. I really think she needs to talk."

"I'd certainly be willing to do so, Brigitte, but she and I have never met each other."

"I know, Bob. But when I offered to help set up a visit with you, she seemed interested."

Within the hour I was on the phone, introducing myself to Janelle. She indicated she was anticipating my call. After a brief exchange we agreed I would come by the following afternoon.

When Janelle opened her front door the next day, she welcomed me in. We proceeded to sit at the family's kitchen table. I immediately noticed two opened tissue boxes sitting squarely in the middle of the table, with a waste basket beside the chair into which Janelle settled. The basket was already close to overflowing.

I began. "I appreciate your willingness to invite me into your home, Janelle, especially considering we've not met before."

"Well, Brigitte thought it would be a good idea for me to talk. She said I could say whatever I wanted to you." Acknowledging her gracious trust in Brigitte's counsel, I expressed my condolences to her on her daughter's passing. On my invitation she then revisited in some detail what had transpired during that week six months earlier. She described everything, from the first indication her daughter wasn't acting quite right, all the way through coming home from the post-funeral reception and walking into her daughter's bedroom and throwing herself onto the empty bed, curling into a ball and sobbing.

I listened, my heart aching. When Janelle quietly ended her description of those first days and weeks, I asked her, "And now. How about now? How are you doing today?"

"Okay, Pastor Bob. You asked? Then I'll tell you. I'm empty. I walk through each day in a dark fog. I try desperately to be there for our son and daughter. My husband, thank God, does far better at that than I." She stopped. I waited. She continued, now with unadulterated intensity, "I'm beginning to learn how cruel people can be without their even knowing it.

When they think they're being helpful, they're not." She wiped a tear away. It wasn't a tear of sadness, but of isolation. "They want so much for me to get on with it. To be happy again."

"How so?"

"They seem to feel that I should be somehow getting over her death." Silence. "It's as though they need me to be done with mourning so they don't have to grieve with me any longer."

"That must hurt. Deeply."

"You have no idea." I didn't disagree. Then she asked me, "May I give you some advice?"

"Of course," I responded, not sure what was coming.

"Never, ever tell someone who's lost a child, 'Well, your daughter's in a better place.'" She stopped. I again waited. "Do you realize how incredibly hurtful and insulting that kind of comment is?" I nodded silently. Angrily she said, "My daughter had a wonderful home with us. She had two amazing parents. A loving older brother. An adoring younger sister. A home where she was our light, our joy." I nodded silently, now feeling her anger myself. "My friends have the gall to tell me that I can take solace in knowing that my daughter's in a better place? No! She was where God wanted her to be. Here! Not ripped away from us. Not leaving us aching to see her every morning, every afternoon, every night, just so that she can be in some 'better place.'"

I nodded again.

"And never, ever tell someone who's lost a child, 'Well, at least you have two beautiful children still in your home.'" Bitterly she explained, "My best friends, the ones I thought knew me and loved me, they say to me, 'Janelle, thank God you still have your son and daughter.' As if the two of them are meant to fill the emptiness?" She wiped her eyes and continued. "Don't ever, ever tell somebody that they 'at least' still have someone else after they've lost a loved one." Now sobbing, she added, "It doesn't work that way. It doesn't work that way."

Our conversation continued. I ended up staying the better part of three hours. There was grief and there was anger. Two souls were bared. No excuses were made. Yet, a bit of salve was felt—by both of us. Though Janelle's emptiness remained, she was not alone in it.

God would have it no other way.

21

It's Bleeding

IT'S FASCINATING WHAT COMES to mind on occasion, including when the extraordinary unexpectedly insists its way into the ordinary.

I had led several worship services for residents of the nearby nursing home, and was doing so again, this time on the Wednesday afternoon of Holy Week. The service, as usual, was unfolding in the small chapel, complete with requisite electric organ, dog-eared non-denominational hymnbooks, interdenominational Communion Table, and somewhat wobbly lectern. Then there was that imposing, lifelike, four foot tall crucifix, hung prominently on the wall immediately behind the Table and lectern.

It was Holy Week, so I had naturally chosen to read a portion of the Good Friday narrative. I was quietly reflecting aloud about the significance of Jesus's crucifixion, so undeniably on display with his body nailed to that cross on the wall. Having that Roman Catholic crucifix close at hand provided me an expository opportunity rarely afforded a Protestant preacher, given the sixteenth century Reformers' insistence that a sanctuary's cross be "empty" of any body hanging on it.

The worshipers were some thirty in number, most all in their wheelchairs. Some had fallen asleep, as was the norm. But many others were clearly awake, giving me a sense my words were not falling on deaf ears.

And what words they were, as I pontificated about Jesus's sacrifice on that cross, to which I would point with outstretched arm in order to make it quite clear about whom it was I was preaching.

Then the extraordinary insisted its way into the otherwise ordinary sermonic moment. While droning on from the lectern, pointing with pastoral care toward the crucifix behind me, I heard a voice. It was male, and it was clear. In fact it betrayed real shock. The voice cried out, "It's bleeding!"

I stopped mid-sentence, mid-sermon. Dead stop, slack jawed. It's *bleeding*? The crucifix's body is bleeding? Without thinking, I whirled sideways, close enough to make a careful inspection of the crucifix. As I was doing so, my Protestant brain silently bemoaned to itself, "I'm not a priest! I know next to nothing about the stigmata, those nail holes in Jesus's wrists that some say they've seen bleeding on crucifixes! How am I supposed to deal with a bleeding crucifix?"

Odd what the mind betrays with its secretive honesty.

From the moment I heard the elderly man's voice announce the bleeding, to the moment I stared in anxiety at that crucifix, two, maybe three, seconds had passed. But what eternally long seconds they were. I stood there, nakedly a *non*-Roman cleric, sweeping the crucifix for evidence of bleeding. And saw none, with the exception of that dry, crimson paint which had been artistically applied by its maker in some woodshop who knows how many years earlier.

No actual bleeding! *Whew!*

But what then of that voice? While I stood there inspecting the crucifix, heaving a quiet sigh of relief, the voice cried out again, now with even more intensity, "It's *bleeding*!"

I quickly turned back toward the wheel-chaired congregants, leaving the wooden crucifix behind. That's when I located the man in his wheelchair. *Ecce homo!* There he was, front and center. But not looking up at the crucifix. Rather, he was staring, wild-eyed, at his left knee. With his left hand holding the pant leg up past the knee cap, his right hand was massaging the injured knee, pointing at the scab that had just let loose. With blood. His own.

I moaned. Partly on the poor gentleman's behalf. But also, truth be told, on my own. In that instant, I'm embarrassed to admit, I sighed in relief. No explanations about the nature of stigmata would be called for.

And yet.

While no words would be called for, my sermonic reflections about Jesus's death, to which I returned as soon as the compromised knee was tended to, demanded of me closer attention. It demanded a deeper consideration of what our Lord's gift on the cross really entailed. What it entailed in all of its bitterly painful, but ultimately life-giving, wonder.

22

Strictly Business

WHO WOULD HAVE THOUGHT that such an iconic statement made by two Mafia dons, played masterfully by Brando and Pacino, would come to mind within the first hour of enduring that intense conversation with my fellow pastor? But it did. "It's not personal. It's strictly business." Those were the cinematic words that hit me. That gave me insight into what had just transpired in my study, leaving me almost speechless.

It all started a day earlier—or, more truthfully, years earlier when I had been a student. As a seminarian I wrestled with any number of long-standing theological positions that have been held by the denomination of my upbringing. One of those positions argues that some within the human family will ultimately be welcomed into eternal communion with our maker, while the rest will not. That is, some will be saved, but none of the rest. I struggled to make sense of that position and its suggested duality of God's redeeming designs, ultimately finding I could not. Rather, convinced of the radical breadth of God's gracious embrace of the whole of humanity, I discovered I was a Christian universalist: I was all in as a believer in the divine's intent to deprive not one single child, woman, or man of eternal life's blessings.

As the years passed my Christian universalist conviction only deepened. Though I didn't widely broadcast this belief, neither did I hide it. So it was only a matter of time before I was invited to share it publicly with my peers in ministry.

Which is how echoes of Brando and Pacino soon presented themselves to me.

I was asked to describe my Christian universalist position during a special evening gathering of ecclesiastical leaders near my home parish. I did so, eliciting several comments and questions immediately thereafter.

But the following morning my phone rang. Joe, a fellow pastor, asked if he could come by and visit with me about my presentation the previous night. I welcomed him, albeit anticipating we would likely find ourselves at odds over my position. But we were friends. I had called on him several times the previous year while he was recovering from major surgery in a nearby hospital. He had even noted I was the only pastor who had come by to see him during that stretch, and he had much appreciated my taking the time to do so.

Though I guessed that Joe's forthcoming visit with me would yield lively, even heated, conversation, I also looked forward to building on our friendship.

So much for my gift of clairvoyance.

Joe knocked on my study door, strode in when I opened it with a smile, and started in before he had fully settled into his chair. "Bob, I'm here to tell you you're wrong. Dead wrong. What you disclosed about yourself last evening was frightfully heretical, and you need to be set right." By instinct and training a listener, I opted to allow Joe the floor. He proceeded to clarify how my Christian universalist position was not just wayward, but endangering to me and anyone else whom I might lead down the same egregious path.

When he came to what appeared to be a stopping point, I said as respectfully as possible, "Joe, if it's okay with you, I'd like to share with you, in a little more detail than I did last night, what lies behind my convictions."

Before I had a chance to proceed, Joe interrupted. "No, Bob. I know exactly what you'd try to tell me. I've read and heard it all before. I don't need to listen to you. I didn't come here to hear you out. I came here to let you know you're wrong." I found myself speechless. Not just because, for all practical purposes, he was insisting I not speak, but because I was totally unaccustomed to being told, "I know exactly what you're thinking. I don't need to listen to you." Joe then reached for his jacket, readying himself for his exit.

Only then did I manage to say, "Joe, I ask that you not leave quite yet. I was hopeful we could talk. I was looking forward to hearing what you have to share with me, and to thinking out loud with you about what my unfolding faith pilgrimage is about."

He looked at me. He smiled. At least I think it was a smile. He said, "There's no reason for me to stay any longer. I've said what I came to say. Good-bye, Bob." With that he walked out of my study. And out of my life. I stood there in my study, immobile. I recall trying to take a few deep breaths before I stumbled back to my desk and flopped into my chair.

There I sat, asking myself, "What just happened here?"

What just happened? A friend came for a visit that, for all practical purposes, amounted to nothing more than—and nothing less than—a browbeating lecture, a biblical scolding, and most troubling, a declaration of separation.

It was a first for me. For a spell I was confounded. How could a friend walk in, attack, and then refuse to listen? For the better part of an hour I sat in a daze, trying to make sense of it all. That's when the dons came to mind. That's when Marlon and Al, playing the screen roles of Corleone father and son in *The Godfather*, presented themselves to me. They looked at me in their patronizing and dead pan manner and declared, "Bob, you need to understand. It's not personal. It's strictly business."

It's not personal. It's strictly business.

As deeply personal as I had thought that interaction with Joe had been, it began to dawn on me Joe had come on business. Joe's worldview—his theological view, if you will—insisted on it. His worldview was rooted in the conviction that dialogue with opposing worldviews is dangerous. What he believed included a requirement he not discuss in an open-minded manner anything with anyone with whom he disagreed, apparently for fear that the opposing position might corrupt, or even obliterate, his correct viewpoint.

Sitting at my desk, I realized the following, which both shook me and shaped me. Joe's worldview was and is entirely different than my own. Joe couldn't converse with someone, even a friend, about opposing faith viewpoints. He couldn't without jeopardizing his own spiritual well-being. He wouldn't for fear of imperiling his very salvation.

In contrast, my worldview insists on conversation with anyone and everyone, friend or otherwise, about opposing faith viewpoints. I can and must, because doing so will enrich my spiritual well-being and will broaden my wonder about the mystery of our very salvation.

When Joe called to say he wanted to come to see me, it wasn't personal. It was strictly business. Not because he was questioning our friendship. Rather, because his worldview, his very theology, demanded he ignore that friendship for the sake of honoring the truth of his worldview, for the sake of submitting himself to the dictates of his faith perspective.

In retrospect it would have been helpful if both Joe and I had been clear and honest about what was happening that morning in my study. Joe, in all good faith, was on a business trip dictated by his faith. Had I understood that, I would have been less vulnerable to taking it all too personally. I could have looked my friend in the eye and said, "Thank you for your honesty and for your faithful execution of what your faith demands of you."

It wasn't personal. He didn't come intent on hurting his friend. He came on a business venture demanded by his own theological convictions. It just happened to be, on that particular day, *I* was on the business end of that venture.

In the years since that last interaction I ever had with Joe, I've had other instances where I've found myself hearkening back to Brando and Pacino. There have been other situations when what has felt like a personal moment has best been diagnosed as a business moment. A business moment demanded, ironically, by someone's faith.

Have those moments been pain-free? No. But my pain has been less confounding to me because I've been able to say, along with Marlon and Al, "Bob, remember. It's not personal. It's strictly business."

In the meantime I also realize my professed conviction about God's universal gift of salvation—which prompted dear Joe to come and give me the business in the first place—remains my conviction: that God will embrace all creation, and everyone in it, for eternity. And that same God insists I remain open to conversation with everyone, including with those whose very faith ironically bars such conversation.

23

Hunger

HER LOOK WAS ONE of both boredom and hunger. Such an odd combination, and yet it struck me her fifteen year old face betrayed both attitudes.

Bridget was sitting amongst a group of eight high schoolers. They comprised that fall's collection of confirmation class participants. It was the end of the second of five scheduled sessions, and I sat at the head of the table as the leader.

This year's class was the fourth such version I had tackled during the first several years in my ministry with the congregation. I had scrambled each year for a curriculum that might connect with that year's class. Thus far I had found myself frustrated by each version. None had grabbed me. And forget the youth themselves. Most attending on the strong—read: insistent—recommendation of their caring parents, they endured my attempts at both education and dialogue. In rare moments a spark of energy or curiosity seemed to be aroused, but only to die out all too quickly in the ensuing exchanges.

Such was the case when I caught Bridget's look. To her everlasting credit, it was clear she was making a cordial effort to hang in with the pastor and his tedious attempts at making the questions and history of the Christian faith at least somewhat interesting, if not magnetically intriguing. She looked me in the eye, and her expression revealed unapologetic boredom. But it also revealed an openness of sorts, a hunger that seemed to say, "Okay, Pastor Bob, I'm game to listen. Do you have anything at *all* I can relate to?"

The next evening I sat in my living room, irritated. Not at Bridget, but at myself and at my church. At myself for feeling an embarrassing incapacity to make the Gospel relevant to teens; at the wider church for failing miserably, in my estimation, in its institutional efforts to produce material that might actually grab the attention and stir the imagination of adolescents sacrificing precious time by attending confirmation classes. Weary of mulling over how to proceed, I surrendered to the moment by opening that month's *National Geographic*. It had arrived in the previous week's mail, and was sitting innocently enough on the table beside my chair. I scanned the cover, which listed the titles of the articles within. One title caught my fancy: *"The Universe,"* Page 63. I flipped to that page, and out fell a map. I plucked the map from my lap, and read, again, "The Universe."

Intrigued, I unfolded the new map. As with so many of its counterparts in other *National Geographic* monthlies, it proved to be remarkably large. No surprise, I suppose. This was the Universe, right? Unable to get a good viewing of the map while seated, I got out of the chair and spread the map on the living room carpet. I carefully smoothed out the creases, and then took in its imaginative presentation.

The cartographer/artist had done what, of necessity, she had to do. She had masterfully created one of those maps-within-a-map that one sees on occasion, where the larger map has a spot within it that needs to be enlarged in order to reveal a site too small to be evident on its own. That spot has an arrow pointing to it, and at the base of the arrow is another map of the small space now enlarged enough to reveal the site in question.

This particular map's designer had used that technique. But not just once, nor twice. She had used it six times! After the sixth iteration of a map-within-a-map, there was the earth, part of our tiny solar system. When I allowed myself to try to fathom what the brilliant cartographer/artist had managed to do, revealing the infinitesimally tiny presence of humanity's earthly home in the infinitely enormous breadth of the known Universe, I quietly whispered, "Whoa."

I had studied and read about the size of the Universe on any number of occasions over the previous decades. But this was the first time I could see with my own eyes, so to speak, what really is beyond our capacity to imagine. There we were, a speck in the breathlessly huge expanse of the Universe.

Then it hit me: God is right here, with us, on this speck; but God is also everywhere else, doing God's creative thing!

God is right here, with me and every other human me, loving and holding and knowing us. But God is also, at the same instant, thirteen billion light years away, loving and holding and knowing everything and everyone else whom God has fashioned!

Before I realized what I was doing, I was praying. Not saying words, nor constructing sentences, but simply letting my spirit both be still and soar. I was allowing the Spirit to utter what is beyond human limitations of wonder and awe.

You can probably guess, fairly quickly, what I realized I could do the following week. Or better, what I realized I had to do. At the start of the third session of the confirmation class, I opened with a brief prayer and then informed the youth we'd be foregoing the outline of material I had distributed at the start of the first session. Instead, we were going to look at a map. The teens stared at me, understandably perplexed. But they then leaned forward, each and every one of them, as I took the map of the Universe, unfolded it, spread it out in the middle of the table, and smoothed out the creases. "What are we looking at?" I queried them.

Brad, typically the most verbal among them, said, "The Universe."

"Yup. Any one ever see this version of a map of the Universe before?" No one responded. "Well, let's take a look at it." No one objected. Instead, to a girl and boy around the table, including Bridget, each craned forward in order to get a better look. I proceeded to explain how to understand the map-within-a-map design, and what it suggested about where our planet fits in the grand scheme of things. After a minute or two of that simple explanation, I sat back in my chair. But no one else did. Instead, each remained bent over the map, taking it all in. Not a word was spoken. But the energy, the curiosity—yes, the awe—became palpable.

"Whoa," said Bridget. I had to smile to myself when I heard her say it. A few echoed her expression. Each did so in a hushed manner.

The holy has a way of eliciting both a sense of wonder, as well as a quieting of person.

The holy has a way of seeding what we all too easily describe as "faith."

The holy has a way of transforming the way we look at our God. At our Universe. At our selves.

The holy has a way of disclosing the undiscloseable.

As you might guess, that evening we didn't return at all to the original curriculum. Instead, we began to explore what it means to be God's. And guess what? Bridget left with a look on her face that suggested a hunger. A new kind of hunger.

24

In the Wake of 9/11

THE STARK CONTRAST BETWEEN the two conversations was totally unanticipated. Yet each conversation had reflected reality in a unique, even painful way.

It was mid-summer of 2003. I was part of a group of a dozen or more volunteers from my congregation. We had driven one hundred and fifty miles south and were staying for six days in the basement of a church on Staten Island, just a thirty minute ferry ride from Manhattan. We were there to offer hands-on assistance with some of the various ministries the host congregation had been providing for decades to the surrounding community. Those ministries included a food pantry, clothing distribution, support for the homeless, and so forth.

But a brand new ministry had taken shape over the previous twenty-two months, as well. It was born out of the horrors of the 9/11 attacks on the World Trade Center. A significant handful of the congregation's members had lost loved ones and friends in the collapse of the twin towers, and the congregation had quickly and compassionately fashioned ways and places to offer support to the victims' grieving survivors. In that context, on the fourth day of the week of our volunteering, the host pastor invited me and two other volunteers to dedicate that afternoon to delivering plates of cookies to two households of relatives who had perished on 9/11. The three of us—two adults and Lana, a teenager—agreed to do so, humbled by the invitation.

The first home was several long blocks from the church building. The twosome we were to call on at that residence included a widowed mother in her late twenties, and her now fatherless daughter, age four. We drove to the address and parked down the street. We walked to the front door of the simple, clapboard house, all three of us hushed in our brief conversation about what lay in store for us. We rang the doorbell and stood back a respectful few feet from the entrance, plastic-wrapped plate of cookies held in plain sight by young Lana. In short order the door was opened. Mother and daughter stood before us, the little one peering at us from behind her mother's legs, to which she was clinging as only a shy child does.

By previous agreement amongst our little visitation threesome, I said, "Good afternoon, Mrs. Smith. We're here on behalf of your home church. My name is Bob, and this is Millie and Lana." She nodded, without saying a word. "We're from a church near Albany, and are doing volunteer work with your church this week. Your pastor asked us to bring this plate of cookies to you and your daughter. It's from the congregation's support team that's been meeting ever since the 9/11 attacks." She nodded again, still remaining silent. Lana extended the plate towards her and her daughter, both still standing in the doorway, neither moving. The young mother took the plate, with a trace of a smile.

"Thank you," she said. Nothing more.

"You're most welcome," I responded. Silence for a few seconds. "We want to offer the two of you our heartfelt condolences on your loss." She nodded a second time, saying nothing. Her lips trembled slightly. "Is there anything that the three of us might be able to do on behalf of you and your daughter?"

She shook her head, glancing down at her daughter, who was looking at the three of us, and then at the plate of cookies now in her mother's hands. "No. Thank you. Very much." Then she immediately said, "I'm afraid the two of us have a busy afternoon ahead of us. Please tell everyone at the church we appreciate being remembered this way."

"Of course. We'll be sure to have your pastor convey that message to the congregation this Sunday." She nodded. "Well, we'll be on our way then." She nodded again. "Please know that your daughter and you have our prayers." Another nod. The three of us stepped back, and she began to close the door. Just before it shut in full, I glanced down and saw the curiosity-filled eyes of her daughter, studying us wordlessly. Matching the child's silence, the three of us walked back to our parked car.

We drove several blocks to the second house assigned to us, saying very little to one another. The quiet felt fitting, given the painful solemnity of the one or two minutes spent in the first home's doorway. This next house, we had been told by the pastor, was home to a couple whose twenty-eight year old son, engaged to be married late in the fall of 2001, had perished when the second tower collapsed.

Once again we parked our car and walked up to the doorway, second plate of cookies in Lana's hands. Again the doorbell was rung. We stepped back a respectful couple of feet. As before, the door opened. This time a slightly graying gentleman stood before us. "Good afternoon, Mr. Jones. We're here on behalf of your home church. My name is Bob, and this is Millie and Lana."

He immediately smiled and responded. "Good afternoon to all three of you. What can I do for you?"

As just a few minutes earlier, I said, "Well, we're from a church near Albany. We're doing volunteer work with your church this week. Your pastor asked us to bring this plate of cookies to you and your wife. It's from the congregation's support team that's been meeting ever since 9/11."

To my surprise, Mr. Jones smiled and said, "Well, how nice of you folks!" Looking back over his shoulder, he called out, "Ginger, we have guests from the church's support team!" To us he then said, "Come in! Please come in!"

The contrast to our experience just ten minutes earlier was jolting. For a moment the three of us stood there, not sure whether to accept his warm, even insistent, invitation. Again he said, with a wide sweep of his arm inward, "Please come in."

"Thank you," we each responded, stepping directly into their living room. As we did so, Mrs. Jones appeared, wiping her hands on an apron.

"Ginger, this is Bob and Millie and Lana. They're here from the church with cookies for us from the support team."

"Oh, do sit down!" Again the three of us betrayed our uncertainty, even timidity. "Sit, sit!" insisted Mrs. Jones. Lana, still holding the plate, extended it to our hostess, who hugged her and declared, "Well, aren't you a dear!"

So we stayed. And we listened. And we learned. The Joneses proceeded to introduce us to their late son. We learned about his joy-filled childhood, his academic and athletic achievements, his work as an accountant with a firm in Tower Two, and even his engagement to a young lady with whom they still remained in close contact. We were slowly escorted around the living room, shown several dozen pictures of their son, from his infancy through young adulthood. Each framed image was accompanied by a detailed memory spun out for the three of us in a parental mixture of smiling gratitude and teary-eyed grief.

A full hour unfolded. It became clear, though unspoken among the three of us, the Joneses were giving us a gift only they could give: an introduction to a beloved son whom they yearned, oh so much, to have others come to know. And in receiving that gift from them, we were returning one in kind: ears and hearts receptive to their gift.

Upon returning to the church building late that afternoon, the three of us began to process the two visits. We agreed the stark contrast between the two conversations was totally unanticipated. Yet each had reflected reality in a unique, honestly painful way. The quietly reserved wife and daughter, and the eagerly storytelling father and mother: each appropriately embodied the imponderable nature of loss. And the three of us who were humbled to spend a moment of our lives with all four? We were transformed, if ever so slightly. Transformed by the grace-filled, healing mystery of shared bereavement, both in silence and in story.

25

There

THANKFULLY I MANAGED TO suppress a guffaw, recognizing in the moment that Cynthia wasn't joking. She was as serious as could be.

I had known Cynthia for the better part of three years. I had been introduced to her by her future mother-in-law, who was a friend of ours. Cynthia had begun to date the friend's son, Ronnie, and they were getting serious about being married. By the end of that year a diamond ring had been offered and accepted, and it was time to start planning a wedding.

A word about Cynthia and Ronnie. While each was somewhat learning disabled, they both managed to find and keep jobs, she part-time at the counter of a local store and he full-time with a construction company. When Cynthia originally approached me about their impending nuptials, her request was a bit unorthodox. "Pastor Bob, we need you to hitch us." It was declared in a simple, heartfelt way that was as sincere as could be.

"I'd be honored to officiate at your wedding, Cynthia. Let's schedule a time for Ronnie, you, and me to get together so we can discuss all the details." Within a week or two I was sitting with the twosome, beginning a fairly simplified version of the kind of wedding planning and pre-marriage counseling I was accustomed to using with other couples.

By the end of the second session I found I was enamored with the two-some. They won me over by their unfiltered honesty and their unarguable desire to make their forthcoming marriage work. In spite of their disabilities, it was clear they were committed to each other and to the prospects of making a good life for themselves.

Their wedding date arrived, and the service unfolded memorably. Cynthia and Ronnie exchanged vows and rings while staring seriously into each other's eyes. Though they did not smile much, there was a tone to the moment that spoke indelibly to the depth of feeling each clearly was bringing to the occasion. When I declared that they were now husband and wife, Cynthia nodded at Ronnie and said loudly enough for everyone to hear, "There." Who could contest such a declaration?

In the months following the wedding I occasionally crossed paths with both Cynthia and Ronnie. When I would ask them how they were doing, responses would include, "Just hummin' along, Pastor Bob." "Right fine." "He's still got a job. Can't argue 'bout that." "She makes fine meals, Pastor Bob." In no instance did I find myself wondering about their well-being.

But then came the day after my summer vacation travels, some two years after the wedding. Home from a trip out of state, I returned to work, only to find a scribbled note on my desk. It read, in a mix of print and script, "Need to tell ya stuff, paster Bob. Signed, Cynthia." I called their home right away. Cynthia answered and said, "Be right there. Okay by you?"

"Of course, Cynthia."

Within a few minutes I heard the church's back door crunch open, and down the stairs to my study plodded Cynthia. Once seated, and before I managed to say more than, "It's good to see you again, Cynthia," she started right in.

"It's Ronnie, Pastor Bob." I nodded. "I need to let you know what happened last week." I nodded again. "He came home from work and told me he's spotted a purty girl. He told me she's purtier than me, and he loves her. He told me he thinks he wants to marry her, and not me."

"I'm sorry to hear that, Cynthia. I—"

But before I managed to continue my pastoral response, Cynthia plowed ahead. "So I says to him, 'She may be purtier than me. But so what? Lotsa girls are purtier than me. Everybody knows that, including you, Ronnie.' And then he says, 'I guess so.' And then he says, 'But I think I love her. She's so purty.'" I nodded, not inclined to interrupt again. "So that's when I decided to tell him."

I nodded. Realizing that Cynthia was now apparently awaiting permission to continue, I asked, "Decided to tell him what?"

Without hesitancy she responded, "I told him to get his head out of his butt." Thankfully I managed to suppress a guffaw, recognizing in the moment that Cynthia wasn't joking. She was as serious as could be. "I told him, 'You're married to me. I'm your wife, and you're my husband. And that's the way it's gonna stay.'" She concluded with a strong nod of her head, up and down, as if again to say, "There."

"Good for you, Cynthia," I managed to say, before she pressed on.

"Just thought I'd better let you know what happened, Pastor Bob."

"I'm grateful that you did, Cynthia." She stared at me. I continued, "And how did the conversation go when you said that to him?"

Sounding surprised I had even asked, she declared, "Well fine, of course. He said, 'Oh, okay. I'll stop loving her and keep loving you, Cynthia.'" She nodded her head up and down, as if *again* to say, "There."

"I'm relieved to hear that, Cynthia. I really am."

"Well, of course you are, Pastor Bob. Why wouldn't you be?" She again seemed genuinely surprised I would need to say such a thing. "So we're good now. He took his head out of his butt, and he loves me. 'Cause he's my husband, and that's what husbands do." And before I had a moment to concur, she stood up, gathered herself, and said, "That's all. Just wanted you to know."

"Thank you, Cynthia. I'm grateful. And relieved."

"Yup," she said. "'Course you are. 'Cause you're our minister." With that she walked out of my study and back to her honesty-filled world. In her wake stood a pastor who was moved, even transformed, by her honesty. By her strength. And by her commitment.

Would that all spouses might have what Cynthia has. And would that all spouses might be what Cynthia is.

And by the way, their marriage remains healthy, years later. They are now parents of four lively, incredibly loved children. Children who are not only bright, but—more importantly—honest, strong, and committed.

26

Room in the Circle

ALWAYS ON THE PROWL for a great idea for the approaching Sunday's children's sermon, I thought I had hit the jackpot. It wasn't from a book or an Internet site, or even stolen from a peer who might have described a success she'd pulled off during a recent service. No, this one simply *came* to me. It had the promising glow of becoming one of those moments when children and adults alike would uniformly cry out, "Aha! I get it!" Then there would be a faint sound of angels above, applauding the moment when the preacher had once again deftly disclosed the Good News in all of its self-evident glory.

Well, all best laid plans and such.

Prior to that Sunday's service, anticipating the regular gaggle of five or six children coming forward at the appointed time during the worship hour, I carefully pre-positioned a stack of ten folding chairs, just in case. The service then unfolded. The "Amen" was said by all at the close of the Lord's Prayer, and I proceeded to summon the typically energized kids forward. As they scampered up to the two steps on the chancel where they customarily sat, I ushered them instead straight to the empty floor area in front of the pulpit, adjacent to the waiting folding chairs. Standing with the sixsome, I asked them boldly, "Do any of you know how to play Musical Chairs?"

Six hands shot up, accompanied by six voices chirping, "Yes! I do! I do!"

Smiling with the assurance I was good to go, I grabbed six folding chairs, opened them, and plunked them down in a circle fit for the ensuing ecclesiastical version of the same game that I had enjoyed so frequently as a child. Each promptly moved to a chair of his or her own, clearly ready to join in a bit of the acceptable roughhousing the game elicits once the music starts and stops.

"Ready?" I boomed. All nodded, mischievous smiles betraying their undeniable eagerness for the ensuing battle for chairs. Thinking it a clever variant for the churchly version of Musical Chairs, I began to sing "Jesus Loves the Little Children." For an instant all six kids stared at their pastor with a bit of disbelief. But quickly thereafter they began to do what the game invited. Marching clockwise around the circle of six chairs, they moved with mounting excitement.

Then, per the great idea that had dawned on me with such unarguable brilliance earlier in the week, I grabbed a seventh folding chair. While still singing that ages old number about our Lord's love for such as these six kids, I added that chair to the circle. To their credit, the now clearly bewildered children kept up the march, circling seven chairs, rather than the five they had rightly anticipated would remain after I should have removed one.

" . . . Jesus loves the little children of the world!" I sang, bringing the musical accompaniment to a close. As if on cue all six jumped into the now expanded circle and grabbed a chair. None was left without a seat. *Au contraire*. The pastor's wisdom was on full and glorious display. It was now The Moment. The Moment when it would be indisputably clear God's family never excludes, but always makes room. Room for anyone and everyone.

"Well, kids, what just happened that was different from when you've played Musical Chairs before?" The parable was now going to speak, even shout, for itself. The "aha" moment had come with the simple question: "What just happened that was different?"

Six hands again shot up without a moment's hesitation. "What a teachable moment," I proudly thought to myself. I scanned all six faces, and opted to point at seven year old Sam, who happened to be visiting that morning with his cousin, a member of the congregation. "Sam, what just happened that was different?" *Say it, Sam! Say it!*

"You sang a church song! I've never had that happen before when I played Musical Chairs," Sam crowed, proud beyond measure.

One of the elderly folks in the second pew guffawed. Several others joined in. After a moment of being struck pastorally dumb, I grinned at the congregation, and then looked back at dear ol' Sam and chimed in, "You're right! I'll bet none of us has ever heard 'Jesus Loves the Little Children' while playing Musical Chairs before!"

No disagreement. None.

And not a single word from the children about that extra chair. It simply sat there, a parable somehow begging to be explained.

Well, all best laid plans and such.

Some forty minutes later, standing at the door and greeting my remarkably patient and good humored parishioners, Sam's aunt came through the line and gave me a reassuring hug. Eyes twinkling, barely able to restrain herself, she assured me, "There's room in the circle for all of us, isn't there. Even for you, Bob! Even for you!"

27

Christmas Sorrow

EVERY MID-DECEMBER SINCE THAT particular year, it unfailingly happens. As Christmas approaches, I remember. I remember, just as I had suggested would be the case for all of us who gathered for the memorial service that December twenty-sixth.

The phone call had come early on the morning of December twenty-second. It was from the funeral home. The funeral director informed me that he had just received news of the death of Wanda, thirty year old mother of two little girls. They had been in a one car crash the previous night. Though the little ones were uninjured, their mother had suffered severe injuries. She had passed away shortly after being rushed to a nearby hospital.

Wanda was the daughter of a long-term member of my congregation. As a teenager she had been a beloved babysitter for our own children. Now as I listened to the funeral director, I sat in shocked silence. The widowed husband was on his way to the funeral home in order to make arrangements. The director reported the preliminary phone conversation with the young widower was pointing to a memorial service the day after Christmas, allowing for attendance by all who were in town for the holiday.

Within the next several hours plans were made. Pastoral visits with Wanda's husband and extended family, as well as with Wanda's mother, unfolded within the next two days. On the evening of the twenty-third I ended up in my study, blank sheet of paper staring at me on my desktop. As oftentimes happened in that study over the years, I looked toward the ceiling and silently intoned, "What now, Lord? What's to be said?" In two days we would be celebrating Christmas. The very next day we would be gathering to mourn the unspeakable loss of a loved one and friend. "What now, Lord? What's to be said?"

Then it came. Like a whisper, more than a bolt. My eyes closed, I began to picture the events around the first Christmas. A vision of two refugees, homeless and desperate on their arrival in Bethlehem, came into focus. One was aching in her swollen condition, already feeling the onset of panic that comes with a mother's first labor pains. The other was fruitlessly begging for someone to take them in before those pains gave way to the birth of a child—his, but not his. I began to feel their paralyzing confusion with the unanswerable questions that defined their fledgling life together. I began to sense their loneliness, as well as the terror that would all too soon grip them on hearing angelic warnings of a tyrant bent on infanticide. I began to be overwhelmed by their agony in having to flee southward toward the frightening unknowns of a foreign land, rather than northward toward the caring embrace of family.

Late that evening the paper on my desk was no longer blank. Instead it flooded over with Christmas pain. With Nativity sorrow. With two refugees' story that paradoxically offers solace to the inconsolable whose own story is one of heartrending loss.

Three days later I stood in the pulpit, looking out over a sanctuary filled with sadness. There sat Wanda's family. All around them, squeezed into every pew, sitting on every folding chair, and standing in every open corner, were those who a day earlier had found that Christmas just wasn't, and would never again be, what our wider culture insists to us that it's all about.

And that's what I addressed. I suggested that for Wanda's family, for her friends, and for all of us who so deeply despaired over her sudden death, Christmas would, and should, never be the same. But I offered the following. Christmas would, and should, be henceforth when the wrenching pain of this annual reminder will be matched by the pain Mary and Joseph had to endure. Matched by two lonely, frightened, overwhelmed parents who embodied the human story we all live—desperate to be held in healing hands while life itself seems to be fractured and hopeless.

Every mid-December since that particular year it unfailingly happens. As Christmas approaches, I remember. I remember, just as I had suggested would be the case for all of us who had gathered for the memorial service that December twenty-sixth. I remember that what we celebrate each Christmas is the presence of Jesus, the one who understands our sorrow. Whose own human mother didn't just bear him, but bore the fullness of human loss. Whose own human father didn't just carry him as an infant, but carried the burden of human isolation.

And every Christmas I now remember not just that one. I also remember all of Wanda's sisters and brothers worldwide, whose pain is healed, in the grand scheme of God's things, solely and fully by that same one.

28

Frozen

IT'S ONLY CONJECTURE, OF course. But with no small measure of comic irony, I've often wondered whether the frigid cold both caused the calamitous moment, *and* saved me from its embarrassing consequences.

It was pushing noon on a Saturday in mid-December in a week that had been unusually challenging. In addition to the normal responsibilities of a few hospital visits, several nursing home stops, weekly preparation for the adult ed class and worship that approaching Sunday, the village's funeral home then called. Twice. Two elderly gentlemen had passed away the previous weekend. Neither was a member of any congregation, but the funeral directors, bless their professional hearts, saw fit to recommend the Reformed pastor to the deceased men's families. I then met with each collection of bereaved relatives, with whom I planned their respective services. Peter's service at the funeral home would be on Friday morning, followed immediately by his interment in a nearby cemetery. Gerald's service and burial were designated for twenty-four hours later.

Friday's gatherings in memory of Peter, both at the funeral home and cemetery, unfolded agreeably, albeit with everyone having to bundle up for the graveside service, given the fast approaching cold front rushing down from the northern reaches of Canada.

That cold front hit with a vengeance Friday night. Come Saturday morning, Gerald's family and friends arrived at the funeral home, layered with coats, scarves, gloves, and hats, and confessing unapologetically about having donned all manner of thermal undergarments. I could well relate, having chosen the same while dressing earlier that morning.

The service unfolded with quiet celebration of Gerald's life. No mention was made of Peter, although I had learned informally the two deceased men had been friends of sorts. Not bosom buddies, but village neighbors, so to speak. Though unaddressed during the service, it was apparent the two extended families knew of their shared losses, which turned out to be of no small consequence at the cemetery thereafter.

Following the benediction and the subsequent paying of respects at the soon to be closed casket, the quietly mourning family and friends exited the funeral home. They clambered into their cars, and then followed in procession behind the hearse. The two funeral directors, Matt and Jack, were both members of the congregation I was pastoring. They were my dear friends, and welcomed me into the hearse to join them in the drive to and from the cemetery. As a threesome we led the procession on the ten mile drive to the small cemetery where Gerald would be laid to rest. Gratefully the hearse's heating system was in good shape, allowing us temporary protection from the temps outside that had dipped to minus five degrees Fahrenheit that morning.

We arrived at the cemetery and exited the vehicle. I stood to the side, pulling my scarf tightly around my face, and then watched as my two dear friends directed the dozen cars that had followed us to park in proximity to the waiting open grave. Then, with the assistance of two cemetery hired hands, each bundled up in one-piece work overalls, the heavy casket was carried and put into its proper place, thereafter covered by a fast-freezing floral spray brought along from the funeral home. Per long honored tradition, I took my place at the head of the casket as the car doors opened and the grieving loved ones slipped and slid across the fast-freezing tundra of the cemetery grounds, gathering in a tight cluster at the foot of the casket.

By the time all were assembled, we were, to a man, woman and child, numbingly frozen to the bone. My eyes let me know they were not happy; they both watered and froze at the same instant. My ears, I suspect, were either ruby red or sky blue; either way, they were developing an attitude of distinct displeasure. My nose? It was letting me know, in no uncertain terms, of its sincerest objection to inhaling any more of this absurdly arctic air.

Then there were my hands. Up to the moment the funeral directors nodded in my direction, with eager insistence I proceed with the committal liturgy, I had kept my gloved paws buried in my coat pockets, right hand holding the small service book from which I would read. I then drew my gloved hands out of their protective sanctuaries. Just as I did so, Nanook of the North chose to let loose with a blast of icy wind that just about knocked to our knees all two dozen of us standing around the casket. If memory serves, there was a collective groan of dismay and alarm.

Not wanting to delay in the least what we were there to do, I began. But in order to do so, I removed my gloves. How else to open my liturgy book and turn the pages? First the left glove. Then the right. Within seconds my fingers locked up into something akin to claws.

It was only later that day it struck me that maybe the frigid cold both caused the ensuing calamitous moment, *and* saved me from its consequences.

I sped through the scripture passages and invited us all to pray. I beseeched the Lord's healing care for all who mourned that morning in that icy setting. Then I did it. I thanked God for the gift of Peter.

Peter. Not Gerald, but Peter, whose casket had been lowered into the ground twenty-four hours earlier.

As soon as Peter's name had fluttered out my frozen lips, my brain did a silent somersault. "Uh-oh. Not Peter. But what's the *right* name? Come on, Bob, what's the right name?" Even though that moment reportedly lasted not more than two seconds, it felt like an eternity. "Please, Lord. Help me to remember," I prayed wordlessly.

Gerald!

"And Lord, just as we all offer you thanks for Peter, we do so now also for the gift of his wonderful neighbor Gerald, who joins Peter in receiving your gracious embrace in heaven."

A muffled chuckle from behind me. Not a gasp. A chuckle. From my two friends. The guys who had suggested my name to Gerald's bereaved family in the first place.

The wind churned all around us. As quickly as possible, I brought the prayer to a merciful end. I offered the prayer of committal and pronounced a quick benediction. I then stepped back from the graveside, allowing my two friends to dismiss everyone to their cars. Several of Gerald's family astonished me by graciously expressing their profound thanks for the service, with not a single word about my having mentioned Peter's name.

Once the dozen cars had departed the cemetery, I retreated to the hearse, deliriously joyful to slam my frozen digits smack up against the heating vents. Meanwhile the casket was lowered into the now hardening soil, and my two friends then joined me in the hearse. Huddled together, we started the drive back to the village. I dared say nothing. But as if on cue, the two of them began to chuckle again. Then the laughter erupted. "Best save I've ever witnessed, padre!" chortled Matt.

"Wow! I thought I'd seen and heard it all before," echoed Jack. "But you pulled that off so smoothly I don't think dear Gerald's clan even caught it!"

It took a few minutes as we drove the ten miles homeward, but my dear friends convinced me I was at liberty to join the festivities. I think I began to smile. Maybe even to laugh. About the cold that caused the calamity, and the same cold that in all likelihood masked its potentially embarrassing consequences.

Henceforth, be it winter, spring, summer, or fall, into my beloved liturgy book the name of every single deceased person has been carefully penciled in, and then erased to make room for the next. On every single page.

29

My Family and Yours

I CONFESS IT: I actually growled. Not loudly enough to be heard by the last folks who had just headed to the church parking lot, leaving me to be the one to douse the lights and turn the thermostat down. But I did growl. In the manner that the psalmist might have suggested was the emotional underpinning of one of those various psalms that never, ever get printed in the back of our hymnbooks. One of those embarrassing psalms in which God is beseeched in raw anger to exact harsh, unflinching punishment on the injured psalmist's enemies. One of those psalms that likely weren't sung in Jerusalem's temple three millennia ago, so much as were shouted or groaned. Or yes, growled.

"If you had first checked with me, Lord, I could have helped you get it right." Growl. "But no, you just did it your way, and now look at the results." Silence. Quieter growl.

For the previous two hours I had done my pastoral best to moderate an insane committee meeting. The gathering had blown up when two of the six present decided to have at it. The agenda suggested that we were supposed to be discussing Sunday school curriculum options, or bathroom paint color possibilities, or who knows what. All that mattered, as I sat pouting at my desk, was that whatever we were tasked to do didn't get done.

It didn't get done because two of them decided to attack each other, leaving three mute, shell-shocked onlookers. And me.

Me. Poor me.

Drawing on all of my pastoral skills and instincts, I had spent more than an hour trying valiantly to help the two individuals listen to each other. To honor their sister and brother with a modicum of respect. To do some constructive work on behalf of the wider church's curriculum or bathroom needs or whatever. But no. Try as I might, the twosome dug down deep to find increasingly sophisticated, even corrosive, ways to attack each other. Listen to opposing views? Please. Give pause to the outside chance that another perspective, much less its purveyor, might be worthy of just a smidge of patient attention? Nope.

Instead, it was a donnybrook. Fought, I began to realize halfway through the mêlée, by a duo that were simply not gifted, not skilled, with the most basic capacity to allow others to have a say. No matter what intervention, clarification, and coaching I tried to bring to bear, nothing constructive was going to come of our deliberations. Deliberations? More like a mud wrestling free for all.

I had finally suggested that we suspend our "discussion," head home for some rest, and prayerfully return the following week in order to work toward a place of compromised-based planning. The silent trio nodded in desperate agreement, and Mr. Hatfield and Ms. McCoy harrumphed their concurrence. A closing prayer signaled general retreat, and now I sat alone in my study, growling.

"If you had first checked with me, Lord, I could have helped you get it right. But no, you just did it your way, and now look at the results." Silence. Quieter growl. "Look at what you've done. Look at the mix—no, the mess—that you've made of this congregation!"

For several minutes I stewed. Then I teared up, exasperated. "Do you see my situation, Lord? Do you see that you've brought together into this little congregation some folks who are grievously wanting? They have virtually no capacity to speak clearly. They seem bereft of any ability to empathize with those they disagree with. They are bent on having their own way, no matter what. No matter what, Lord." Now I groaned. "If you had first checked with me, I could have brought together a healthier collection of believers than you have."

Silence.

Then I saw them. Hanging on the far wall of my study, where I had hung them several years earlier when moving into that sometimes-holy, sometimes-not office, I saw the three framed photos. Of my grandfathers and of my father. All posed in their pastoral manner, decades and decades earlier when they, too, had sat in studies like this. And had likely groaned, and even growled, like the third generation was now doing.

I stared at the faces of Grandpa, Grandpa, and Dad. Then I heard them. Deep within my soul, if I can describe the indescribable in such a clichéd way, I heard them say, "Yes, it's hard. It's not even fair." Then: "You're not alone, you know. You're heard, and not primarily by us."

I sat there, and then the sobs came. I shook, but not in loneliness. Rather, in that moving awareness when one realizes that one is understood, is embraced, is allowed to be hurt, angry, and overwhelmed.

I stared into the three still faces looking gently out at me from the past, as well as from the present. Then I felt it, more than heard it: "I could have asked you, Bob. And I'm sure you could have tried to build my church in a way that would seem better, healthier, than what I've done. But this is what my church is. This is who my church is. This is my family—*and* yours." I now found myself looking not at the three photos, but at the small olive wood cross hanging on the wall facing me. "This is our family. Be their pastor, their friend. Be especially the one who is needed not just by the quiet threesome, but by the quarreling twosome." Silence. "I brought you here for them."

By now the sobs had ended, I realized, and so had the growls. In their place, a stillness, even peace. Not because all was well, but because I was not alone, and because I was not in control. Because I was in the good, mysterious hands of someone whose designs for fashioning the church were graciously and gratefully way beyond my understanding.

And that was okay. That was, in fact, good. Very good.

30

Hallelujah for Organists

No one in the life of a congregation does more for less in thanklessly fulfilling her or his weekly ministry than its organist. No one. All it takes is for the organist's occasional vacation to roll around for that truth to raise its churchly head.

There was that one Christmas Eve, for example, when the guest organist arrived a tad late for warm-up time with the choir, who were already sitting patiently in their seats in the loft. In he strode, primly regaled with black suit, black cummerbund, black bow tie, black walking stick tucked deftly under his left arm, and black cape sweeping behind him. Oh, and with spotless white gloves still protecting his precious hands. With a flourish that would have made Liberace blush, he jauntily ascended the three steps into the loft, bowed majestically to the now wide-eyed choir members, elegantly swept out of his cape, and primly removed the gloves, one digit at a time. The entire bass section looked from him to me, jaws dangling. One of them, I'm still convinced, boldly smiled at me with incisors exposed, vampire-like. Carol singing was, how to say it, *unique* that holy Eve.

But then there was that mid-summer wedding weekend. Oh, now that was when I crossed the Rubicon in total conviction our dear organist was worth well more than her weight in ivory.

The substitute organist and I met for the very first time thirty minutes before the Friday evening rehearsal. I handed her a word by word transcript of the service, including notes intended to cue her for the prelude and processional, as well as the recessional—Bach's *Jesu, Joy of Man's Desiring*. During the ensuing rehearsal she seemed to manage agreeably, including her timely start-up of the recessional each time I walked the young couple through the closing prayer and subsequent benediction. Upon the closing "Amen," she made Bach proud with her entry timed nicely to match the couple's kiss and subsequent descent from the chancel and down the center aisle.

But then Saturday arrived. With the sanctuary now full, all went well through her playing of the prelude. On my cue she transitioned beautifully into the processional, timing Vivaldi's *La Primavera* perfectly. The liturgy unfolded as planned, with bride presented, scripture read, vows exchanged. All that remained were the prayer of blessing on the union, the presentation of husband and wife to the assembled congregation, and the benediction. Everything was going quite smoothly.

Until that "Amen."

I had just beseeched divine blessing on the union, preparing to introduce the couple to everyone. I ended the prayer with the prescribed "Amen." But before I could finish saying, "I now joyfully present to you—" Bach's melody erupted from the organ pipes behind me: *Bah*-da-*dah*-da-*dah*-da-*dah*-da-*dah*-da . . . For an instant I stared in confusion at my liturgy book, wondering what was happening. Just as quickly, I realized that the sub, sitting in the organ pit out of view and immediately behind me, was playing the recessional prematurely. I turned, and over my shoulder I stage-whispered in a voice just loud enough to be heard over the joyous melody of *Jesu, Joy of Man's Desiring*, "Not yet, please. We're not done."

Peering now over her shoulder, looking me straight in the eye, she clearly got the message. Then: *Onnggnngg* . . . The organ died out, mid-chord, sounding awfully like an over-sized, howling cat had just been whacked off of its fence perch and wasn't sure how to stop entertaining the neighbors. The fast dying organ resonance ended, and just as I then collected myself enough to try once again to introduce the newly wedded couple, a voice from the organ pit. Not dainty, mind you. Actually, nothing if not strident: "But you said to start after the 'Amen.'"

How does one argue with what is both right and wrong at the same time? All I could muster, now increasingly hot under my clerical collar, was again to whisper, "The *next* 'Amen', please." No response. Which allowed me to get on with introductions, and then swim desperately for shore, declaring, "Receive now the benediction."

Duly blessed, all heard me end with an "Amen!" On cue, the couple kissed each other. And on cue, from the organ pit, with a sneer that I swear awakened the nocturnal owl who legendarily hung out in the church's bell tower, the sub inquired, "*Now?*"

Over the last few years prior to my retirement, much energy was fruitlessly given to trying to figure out how, oh Lord, I might be able to convince the governing board to re-write our amazing organist's contract so as to forbid her any vacation time. At least, please, until I had retired.

31

The Only One

As I TURNED INTO the small cul de sac, I carefully took my foot off the gas. There in front of the house at the end of the street were parked, in haphazard manner, three police cars and a hearse. Right in front of Lawrence's small house. It was not a scene I expected to encounter. Yet a part of me sighed in quiet recognition of the sad reality that now likely awaited me inside that house.

I had known Lawrence for well more than a decade. Just a couple of years older than I, he had retired prematurely from his job with a local university. On fulltime disability due to an overwhelming combination of ailments and incapacities, he had just recently moved from his sizeable home a few blocks from the church building to a nearby town that offered less expensive housing. Long ago sadly divorced, a father of an only son, and soon to be a first time grandfather, Lawrence had tried to settle into his smaller rental with the stated goal of making a new life of it. But the arthritic pain and severely compromised breathing he endured on a daily basis were clearly taking their toll. On my every other weekly visits with him, be it all too frequently in the hospital or in between in his new home, Lawrence unguardedly disclosed his depression, bordering on despondency. Though he never verbalized in my presence his consideration of suicide, that option felt to be not far from the surface of many of our conversations.

I now slowly pulled up behind the hearse and parked. Two uniformed officers were standing on the front lawn, arms folded, staring at me as I got out of the car and started walking toward them. "Good morning, officers."

"And you are?" asked one of them.

"I'm a pastor. Lawrence's pastor." They nodded grimly, looked at each other briefly, and then the second one instructed me to accompany them into the house. "May I ask what's happened?" I queried as we walked up to the front door. No answer. The first officer held the door for me and nodded for me to enter. I did so, and immediately bumped into two funeral home workers, quickly identifiable by their dark suits and the gurney alongside of which they were standing.

Another uniformed officer approached me. Echoing his partner, he asked, "And you are?"

"I'm a pastor. I came to see Lawrence."

He nodded. "Lawrence is dead. He shot himself last night." I must have groaned, or at least displayed my shock. "I'm sorry, Reverend." I must have nodded, but don't recall saying anything. I had never walked into a comparable setting. I remained wordless. "So you knew him well?"

I must again have nodded. "I've been his pastor for several years. More than ten, actually." Then it hit me. His son. And his pregnant daughter-in-law. Without thinking, I asked, "Officer, do you know if his family has been notified?"

"Didn't have to be. His son is the one who found him this morning and called us. He just left a few minutes ago." I must have nodded again, but said nothing. "You probably want to say a prayer, Reverend? Most priests do after a suicide."

Feeling now a disabling mix of shock, grief, and even a little anger, I managed to mumble, "Uh, yes, thank you."

"I should explain before you go in there. He wrote a note for his son and left it on the bedside table." He stopped. Then he continued, "He didn't want his son to have a big mess to clean up, so he wrote he had decided to shoot himself through the heart, instead of in the head. No brain splatter. And very little bleeding out." I must have nodded dumbly again. "Just thought you should know before you pray and all." He then ushered me into the bedroom. A man in a suit, possibly a detective, was sitting on a chair near the bed, talking quietly on the phone.

There was Lawrence, only his head now visible above a large sheet covering the bed and his body. A little blood had soaked through the sheet, but otherwise, just as Lawrence had apparently promised his son, there seemed to be little else out of the ordinary. His face was surprisingly serene, with the lids now shut over his eyes. The man on the phone looked up at me, nodded, and continued his hushed phone conversation. I stood at the head of the bed and reached for Lawrence's face. I honestly don't recall how long I stood there, but in due course I whispered a prayer. "Lord, Lawrence is in your hands. Hold him. Embrace him. And Lord, do so with his son and daughter-in-law, as well."

Five minutes later I was on my way. Within two hours I was with the grieving couple for whom I had just asked divine support. Lawrence's son was understandably distraught, both with grief and with rage. The mix of sadness and anger made for an inevitably complex conversation, unique in some ways in comparison to every other pastoral encounter I had had up to that point in my experience of ministry.

Five days later the sanctuary was full, which was to me in some ways surprising, if not discomfiting. Lawrence had had, for all practical purposes, few remaining friends in his later years. In some measure because he had cocooned himself in his home, and in some measure because many had drifted away after his divorce, he had lived his last years in relative isolation. But now, following the shocking reality that his life had come to a premature end, many former neighbors and coworkers from past decades opted to attend his funeral.

I've often wondered since then whether some if not many of those individuals in attendance had chosen to be present in order to "find out." Sadly, I believe, suicide is one of those grievous circumstances in our culture which invites almost voyeuristic curiosity. If any were indeed present to satisfy their curiosity, they departed disappointed. With no argument from me, Lawrence's son insisted no mention of suicide would be made during the service. Absent any such reference in the obituary, as well, few if any came to know with certainty how Lawrence's life so abruptly ended.

I may well be unfair in my critique of those who chose to attend Lawrence's service. I actually hope I am. I sincerely hope the dismaying act of suicide is not some odd freak show that draws a tititlated crowd. Rather, for me it is a jarring, distressing reminder of the depth of pain that presses in on the flesh and soul of so many all around us everyday. Did I—can I—accept Lawrence's choice to end his own earthly life? I was, and remain, reminded that that is both the wrong, and the unanswerable, question. What matters in the beginning, and in the end, is that we are meant to be with and for one another, especially in the suffering that universally defines the human pilgrimage.

I miss Lawrence greatly. I know his son and daughter-in-law do, profoundly. And I trust their child, now in her teens, has images of her late grandfather that are life-giving.

But as much as I miss Lawrence, I rejoice he is now free of the pain that so much disrupted his daily existence. I celebrate he is in the healing, compassionate embrace of the only one who truly understands.

32

Sanctuary of Surprise

IT DOESN'T TAKE LONG for a pastor to discover how a worship space can be remarkably meaning-filled. Over the course of each calendar year, that space inevitably becomes the memorable site of any number of holy moments. Those moments will often include the heartwarming, candle lit Christmas Eve service; the tear-inducing Memorial Day Sunday reading of the names of those in the church family who have passed away during the previous twelve months; or the quiet singing of "Were You There" during an ecumenical Good Friday service.

But just as there are those holy times when all seems right in the sanctuary, there are exceptions. Oh, are there exceptions.

It was warm outside, and it felt comparably so inside the church building that late spring afternoon. Some one hundred of us were gathered to celebrate the life of a dear member who had passed away four days earlier. Her extended family had traveled at great length to join many local friends and loved ones in order to celebrate her life. In the first six pews immediately in front of the pulpit sat the assembled ranks of her relatives. Squeezed into those pews, shoulder to shoulder, sat young and elderly alike. Their affection for their departed relative shone unmistakably, with tears and smiles intermingling as I eulogized the dear soul.

I was nearing the end of my fifteen minutes of reflection, standing behind the pulpit and looking compassionately into the eyes of those forty or so family members in the first six pews. Then something happened that jolted all of us. *Whoooommpp!* A rumble rolled through the air. It sounded to my shocked ears as though it had come from the second or third pew right there in front of me.

I stopped mid-sentence. I stared, I'm sure with eyes far wider open than is my wont, right at the folks in the third pew, whose own eyes were uniformly bugging out as first they looked at me, then down at their shoes, and then toward one another to their right and left. Jaws sagged in evident confusion.

An odd silence fell over all of us. It seemed as though no one knew what had just happened, though clearly everyone knew *something* had. Dumbly, I asked the poor folks sitting in those first pews, "Is everyone okay?" Heads slowly began to nod "yes," albeit with accompanying looks of bewilderment, if not uncomfortable uncertainty.

So what's a preacher to do? Plow on through, I slowly decided. I continued my final remarks about the dearly departed, all the while keeping half an eye on the confused worshipers in the third pew. Gratefully nothing else intruded on the service. Within ten minutes the closing hymn and prayer unfolded. I extended to everyone an invitation to head after the service into our fellowship hall for refreshments, and then pronounced the benediction, a bit more brusquely than usual, given my growing sense of urgency to clear the sanctuary.

As the organ postlude was played, probably at a quicker tempo than its composer intended, all the relatives in the first six pews shuffled out. Or, more to the point, scrambled out, none too unhappy to retreat from the sanctuary. Everyone else then proceeded with, shall we say, alacrity to the fellowship hall. I in turn retreated with quiet urgency to my study in order to remove my robe and then head to the cranky door that allowed entry into the basement beneath the one hundred and fifteen year old sanctuary. Just as I managed to hang up the robe, there was a quiet tap on my study door. There stood a middle aged man—a nephew of the deceased, I quickly learned—looking a wee bit distressed. Well, not just a wee bit. "Reverend, you'd best check the church basement."

"Just what I was gonna do."

"Good," he said. "And you'd best be careful." He looked me in the eye. "You see, the floor beneath the third pew, where my wife and I were just sitting, dropped a good three inches during the service."

Oh. My.

We simply stared at each other, clearly feeling the weight of the moment. We then moved—well, raced—back up to the sanctuary, ensuring that everyone was moving out. Once the space was emptied, we parked one of the funeral directors at the door, instructing him to bar re-entry until we could inspect below.

On our way down the nephew noted, to my relief, that he was an engineer by training. I gladly opened the basement entryway door, and stepped aside as he led me in. Within two minutes he had found the culprit. A two foot long crack in one of the main, nine inch by nine inch support beams smiled cruelly at the two of us. The engineer moved his finger through the crack, patting it every which way. He then calmly said, "You might want to get that addressed. Soon."

I nodded vigorously in agreement.

Twenty-four hours later, after an architectural firm had come and done its professional thing, safeguarding the building against any further whoooommpps, I discovered an unconscious shimmer—okay, it was a full-fledged shake—in my hands. The gravity of the moment had begun to sink in. And a sense of the holy—of the holy's protective presence the previous afternoon—washed over my somewhat troubled heart.

Then there was, in contrast to this jarring episode, that other instance when an unexpected, but equally understandable, declaration was made that any other place was preferable to our otherwise meaning-filled worship space. It was another instance when the sanctuary felt like anything but a place of refuge.

Mid-June had arrived. It was the Sunday when each year our congregation soaked in the beauty of a service led primarily by the adult choir, with an assortment of anthems and readings throughout. As such it was a service that attracted large numbers of worshipers. The sanctuary was nearly full. Jack and his beloved wife of well more than half a century were seated toward the back, far from their normal spots near the front. Just beside them happened to be seated Phil, one of three undertakers on our church's membership roll.

We were midway through the worship hour. While the choir was catching their collective breath, I had just finished leading the congregation through a responsive reading of a psalm. Then to my alarm Phil stood upright in his pew and said aloud with some urgency, "Jack. *Jack.*" Phil bent down and disappeared behind the pew in front of him. He then stood and said aloud, "We need some help here. With Jack," he clarified.

Within moments at least five women and men bolted from their various seats around the sanctuary. Those nearest to where Jack was now slumped down on his pew moved out of their seats in order to make way for the first-responders. With robe fluttering behind me as I ran from the pulpit, down the center aisle and toward the frenetic scene, I watched as the responders began to do their professional thing. Two nurses, one physician, and two EMTs took charge. Jack was lugged, unconscious, from his pew to the back of the sanctuary, where he was laid flat on the carpet. Once it was determined that he had arrested, CPR was begun. A 911 call was made.

As I watched from the outer circle of those tending to Jack, I had a distinct sensation prayers were being lifted up all around me. Then Jack's body responded. His arms moved and his head shook back and forth. The EMT and nurse who had taken charge halted their treatment. Gratefully, Jack, with his wide-eyed wife watching nearby, then awakened. He looked around in a daze and asked, "What? What's happening?"

The nurse, smiling, said gently to him, "You've just blacked out a bit, Jack. But it's good to be talking to you."

Jack looked up at all the faces looking down at him, and then he spotted undertaker Phil. "What are *you* doing here?" A number of folks smiled, while one of the EMTs pulled on Phil's sleeve and quietly suggested that it might be best for funeral directors not to be seen hovering over a man who had just arrested. Phil nodded, smiled, and melted back into the circle.

Jack, understandably befuddled, looked around and asked where his wife was. The second nurse, who had been holding her in a comforting embrace, ushered her to the center of the circle, where she managed to kneel down next to her beloved husband. They took each other's hands and looked at each other with an indescribable affection. "You're okay, Jack. You're okay," she said.

"But where am I?" inquired Jack, looking at all of us hovering over him.

"You're in church, Jack."

Then, eliciting a wave of quiet chuckles, he declared gruffly, "Well, I don't ever want to come back *here* again!"

True to his word, he never did. Until the very holy gathering, two years later, when we all celebrated his life, fully lived.

33

Rooster Call

BEING SURPRISED BY THE Spirit is one thing. Being surprised by a rooster was quite another.

For many if not most in the wider Christian populace, Maundy Thursday evening worship is fraught with sober meaning. It invites everyone to accompany Jesus from the quiet upper room, into the shadowed Garden of Gethsemane, through the threat-filled courtroom of the Sanhedrin, and ultimately into the brutal presence of both Herod and Pilate.

That year I had once again carefully designed the flow of the evening's service to include multiple scripture readings describing what Jesus endured as he moved closer and closer to his Friday morning sentencing to die on a cross. Upon the reading of Jesus's arrest the sanctuary lights were dimmed, leaving the congregation in the dark, save for the light from thirteen candles on the chancel. As I read of the Garden betrayal by Judas, the first of those candles was dramatically extinguished. Then, when the Gospel writer noted tragically that the other disciples had fled the scene of Jesus's arrest, another ten were snuffed out. That left still lit only two candles, standing side by side: Peter's, close by that of Jesus.

I proceeded to read the gut-wrenching passage detailing the perjured accusations being hurled at Jesus while in the presence of the high priest. In doing so I also read about Peter, who had snuck quietly into the courtyard just outside of the Sanhedrin's entryway, hoping against hope to see his master be released rather than convicted. I read aloud about Peter's first denial of knowing Jesus, followed by his second. I continued, "Then about an hour later still another kept insisting, 'Surely this man also was with (Jesus); for he is a Galilean.' But Peter said, 'Man, I do not know what you are talking about!' At that moment, while he was still speaking, the cock crowed." (Luke 22:59–60)

I took a breath, ready to continue the reading. Then as if on cue, from somewhere out there in the darkened pews, a voice let loose with a piercing "Cock-a-doodle-*doo*!"

"Wait! *What?*" I thought silently to myself. Dead stop. I looked up from the large Bible from which I had been reading. I stared into the darkly shadowed mix of faces in the sanctuary. I can't attest to it, but I still today suspect that my mouth was suspended in wide open surprise.

"That wasn't part of the plan," I thought to myself. "*Was* it?" Absolute, total confusion. But there it was: a rooster, crowing at the very moment just described in the text.

I honestly have no recollection as to how long everything remained in suspended animation. Two seconds? Ten seconds? Who knows?

But what to do, other than to proceed? So I continued, albeit while truly and utterly in the dark, "The Lord turned and looked at Peter. Then Peter remembered the word of the Lord, how he had said to him, 'Before the cock crows today, you will deny me three times.' And he went out and wept bitterly." (Luke 22:61–62) Still confounded beyond words, I returned to my carefully designed script. I took two steps away from the pulpit and proceeded to snuff out Peter's candle, leaving now only the last candle still lit, that of the betrayed Jesus. Even all these years later, memory tells me echoes of the crowing rooster still hung in the air of the now almost pitch dark sanctuary. And I had no idea what had just happened. None.

Soon the service drew to its dramatic end. The last candle was extinguished with the reading of Jesus's death on the cross. All were invited to leave in silence.

For more than two full days I lived with my confusion, with that surprise that had bordered on unadulterated shock. My ever-patient wife and I tried to process the rooster's mysterious intrusion on the service. Neither of us had any idea who had crowed. Most irrationally and most unsettling of all, I actually began to wonder if anyone present really *had* crowed.

Finally Easter morning arrived. While the sanctuary-packed worship service unfolded with great celebration, I confess to having had a tinge of nervous anticipation that some additional, unscripted intrusion might again erupt—maybe during the reading of how the women found the tomb empty? Thankfully all went as planned. No roosters crowing; no women crying out in amazement.

Following the benediction I walked to the main door and stood, per usual, to greet folks as they departed for home. Person after person, family after family passed by, exchanging Easter greetings with me. Then Bert, a young father, grabbed my hand, inquiring without warning: "So, Bob, what did you think?"

"Good morning, Bert. Happy Easter, Phyllis," I added to his young wife, standing alongside of Bert and holding their slumbering infant son. Looking back into Bert's eager eyes, I said, "I'm not really sure what you're asking about, Bert."

"You know!" he chirped. "On Thursday evening? The rooster?"

Oh.

"You. *You're* the one," I silently thought.

I tried to keep smiling. "So that was you, Bert? You crowed?"

"Yup! So what did you think?"

To myself: "Careful, Bob. You're a pastor. You're *his* pastor. He clearly did what he thought would be helpful, *didn't* he?" I then managed to say, "Well, Bert, it sure was a surprise."

"Exactly, Bob! It was a surprise!" With that, Bert pumped my hand, still in his, and said with pure delight, "Happy Easter! To all of us!" He then passed on by and out the door.

As she followed her husband, Phyllis glowed as she declared, "Isn't he the best?"

"Uh, you're *her* pastor, too, Bob," I thought. I then confessed aloud, "It's hard to argue with you, Phyllis. Happy Easter to all three of you!"

Twenty-four hours later, still trying to process what had happened that Thursday evening, I let myself hear again what Bert had explained to me on Easter: "Exactly, Bob! It was a surprise!"

Huh. He was right, of course. As disruptive as his intrusion on my well-scripted readings had been, the crowing had accomplished its purpose. It had truly, shockingly done to me—maybe to all of us in that sanctuary—what the original rooster's cry had done to Peter.

Maybe, just maybe, I had been surprised not just by the rooster. Maybe I had been surprised, like Peter, by the Spirit, who chose to work through, of all people, Bert.

34

Shocking Gratitude

IT WAS NOT THE first time, and it would not be the last. But it turned out to be unique, nonetheless.

Victoria asked me what I thought she should do, given her husband's slow but steady slide toward his death. Riley was in his early eighties and had been diagnosed with end stage cancer several weeks earlier. Victoria had done all she could in caring for him at home, until his needs clearly exceeded her capacity to tend to him on her own. Her two daughters, who each lived a full day's drive away, had made the long treks to assist in their beloved father's homecare, but had to return to their own families and jobs. That had left Victoria on her own at home with Riley. Riley's oncologist finally convinced Victoria the compassionate choice, both for her and her husband, was to admit him to the in-patient Hospice unit in the hospital where he had received superb out-patient care over the previous months.

Riley had now been a patient in his own private Hospice room for five days. He was so heavily medicated for his excruciating skeletal pain that he was, for all practical purposes, sleeping full-time. Unable to take fluids, it was clear he was close to the end. Understandably Victoria wanted to be with him, day and night. Sleeping in a lounge chair carefully positioned right beside Riley's bed, Victoria had remained with him for five days running.

During that stretch I had twice daily driven to and from the hospital in order to call on the couple. I was profoundly touched by the deep affection on display, Victoria holding the hand of her unresponsive beloved, hardly for a moment ever leaving his side. But, as was evident to the Hospice staff, Victoria's exhaustion was taking its toll.

On arriving for my late afternoon visit that fifth day, I found Victoria now accompanied by elder daughter Susanna. Victoria's head was sagging forward on her chest, with her hand still gripping Riley's. I stood in the doorway for a moment, not wanting to startle Victoria. Susanna waved me in with a warm smile and said, "Look, Mother. It's Pastor Bob." Victoria lifted her head and nodded at me as I came in. "We can ask Pastor Bob, Mother."

I walked into the room and stood bedside, opposite where Victoria was still holding on dearly to her husband, with their daughter now rising to stand beside her mother.

"Susanna. Victoria." I looked each in the eye and then bent over Riley and said quietly, "Riley, it's Pastor Bob." As anticipated, he remained silent, shallow and slow breath betraying his precarious condition. While rubbing Riley's boney shoulder, I looked back at mother and daughter. "Susanna, I'm glad you were able to make it all the way back here again." Susanna nodded, smiling weakly, rubbing her mother's shoulder. "Any changes with Riley since this morning, Victoria?"

She shook her head slightly, looking down at him. Looking back up at me, she said quietly, "No. The same, but weaker." I nodded. She then glanced at Susanna, who tilted her head toward me, then gesturing to her mother to go on. "The staff here: they think I should go home and get a good night's rest." She looked down at Riley. "They're concerned that I'm going to fall apart or get sick or something, if I stay here through one more night." She looked back at her daughter. "And Susanna agrees." Susanna teared up and nodded. "So I'm trying to decide what to do. I want to stay here and not leave Riley alone. But I'm exhausted." She then looked up at me, asking, "What do you think I should do? Should I stay or should I go home for the night?"

This wasn't the first time that I'd been asked that question in comparable circumstances, nor would it be the last. But this time it turned out to be unique. I responded, "How do you feel about the options, Victoria?"

She shook her head back and forth. "Well, I don't want to leave him alone. But I think I do need some good sleep in a bed." She looked toward the door. "The staff are very caring. They stop in to check on Riley every ten or fifteen minutes. They assure me that it'll be fine if I go home. So that's what I'm thinking of doing." Glancing at Susanna, she continued. "She'll go with me to make sure I get home safely." To Susanna she asked, "And we'll come back first thing in the morning?"

"Of course, Mother."

"So what do you think, Pastor Bob? Do you think it'll be okay if I leave Riley for the night?"

I hesitated for just a moment. I then answered, "Given what you've told me, Victoria—that the staff will be checking on Riley, and that you and Susanna could both use a good night's bed rest—yes, I think it makes sense for you to go home tonight."

She nodded slowly, looking down at Riley. "Okay." To her daughter she said, "Maybe around 9:00 o'clock?"

"Whenever you're ready, Mother." After a few more minutes of quiet bedside conversation, I prayed with all three and excused myself.

The following morning I arrived at the Hospice unit at 8:00 o'clock. Exiting the elevator I walked to the end of the hallway and entered Riley's room. He was alone, as I anticipated might be the case. I moved to my familiar spot bedside, taking his hand, which was now even more cool to the touch than the previous afternoon. "Riley, it's Pastor Bob again." His eye lids, long shut, quivered. I watched his chest. It rose ever so slightly. "Riley, I'm going to have a prayer with you." I did so. I then stood quietly, holding his hand, watching for another breath. One came. Then a second. I waited for the third. And I waited. Nothing. "Riley?" I asked quietly. "Riley." Nothing.

Oh no.

I waited for another two minutes. Then I walked quickly out to the nurses' station. "Nurse, would you please come and check on Riley."

"Of course, Pastor." We walked back down to the room. She bent down over Riley, checking for a pulse. She pulled her stethoscope from her pocket, checking again. "I'm sorry, Pastor. He's passed."

I stood stock still, both sad and distressed. Victoria. And Susanna. At home. "Nurse, have Riley's wife or daughter been here yet this morning?"

She shook her head. "No. You're the only one who's been here since they went home late last night." She proceeded to straighten the sheets, valiantly making things as peaceful in appearance as possible. "I'll go down to the station and give them a call."

She left the room. I stood there, bedside, looking down at dear Riley, both beginning to deal with my own grief, but also beginning to image what lay immediately ahead with Victoria and Susanna's impending arrival. I stood quietly beside the bed for five minutes, then decided to make a call to the church in order to alert my office administrator. I exited the room, head down, and began the short walk back toward the nurses' station. I looked up as I went. And there they were, just getting off the elevator. Mother and daughter, arm in arm. I stopped, as did they for a moment. We then started walking toward one another. Before I managed to say a word, Victoria spoke. "Is he gone?"

I nodded. "Yes, Victoria. I'm sorry. Not even ten minutes ago." Looking at both of them I said, "I'm so sorry for your loss."

But this was the moment that then made it all so unique. Beyond predictable. "Were you with him, Pastor Bob?" asked Victoria.

"Yes, I had just arrived and had a prayer with him. He took two more breaths and then he passed." They looked at each other, then back at me.

"So you were with Dad when he died?" asked Susanna.

"Yes."

We stood silently as a threesome for several seconds, when the following caused my heart to melt. Victoria said, "Oh, Pastor Bob. I'm so, so relieved you were with him at the end." Tears flowed down her cheek. "It was meant to be this way." She then let go of her daughter's arm and proceeded to embrace me, arms folded tightly around my torso. "Thank you, thank you, thank you."

I was speechless. One minute I was shot through with anxiety that their arrival and discovery of Riley's passing would elicit regret and anger. The next minute I was on the receiving end of a spirit of grace and gratitude that defied description.

I hugged Victoria back. Then Susanna. We then all walked together into Riley's room. We stood bedside, mother and daughter each taking a hand of their beloved. On their request I offered thanks to the God of life that Riley's suffering was behind him, and asked for healing peace for his family. A few minutes of quiet conversation passed. I then departed, but not before each of them, far better perceiving the divine hand in the previous hours than I had, expressed again their gratitude that I had been there in their stead.

A unique, unanticipated blessing. A sadness boundlessly redeemed by gratitude.

35

To Hell and Back

IT WAS THE SADDEST "of course" I had ever said, or will likely ever say again. I hung up the phone a few moments later and then sat at my desk, in a fog. "Lord," I mumbled, "what have I gotten myself into?" Well, I knew the simple answer to that question. It was all that came *with* that simple answer that was giving me pause.

Nikki had called ten minutes earlier. As was the case with countless other phone exchanges with her over the previous four months, she had been grievously despondent. This time that despondency framed her request I drive the one hundred forty miles to her son's sentencing, and then to drive that same one hundred and forty miles back home without that son.

The chain of events leading to this moment was, like most chains, defined by the unexpected. Two years earlier I had received a phone call from Nikki, a member of a neighboring parish. I had come to know her, in part because she regularly attended an ecumenical study group I hosted monthly. "I know this is peculiar, Pastor Bob," Nikki began. "But I'm calling about my daughter and her fiancé. They're scheduled to be married at a nearby community hall in three weeks, but they now need someone to officiate." She explained how the clergyperson who had originally agreed to do so had backed out, leaving the couple high and dry.

Three weeks later the couple stood before me, exchanging vows in the presence of friends and family. Standing as a member of the wedding party was the bride's younger brother. Curt had been an Eagle Scout in high school and was now a successful undergraduate in a small college three hours from home.

Less than two years later life came apart for Curt and his entire family. A week before his commencement exercises, Curt joined a number of college pals at a frat house bash. Men and women shared in the end of college festivities. Alcohol was consumed. Curt, blindly inebriated, trailed an equally drunk coed into a bedroom, where the unspeakable unfolded. The following day, when it became clear to Curt what he had done, he wrote a letter of apology to the young woman. He was arrested later the same day. Two days thereafter he was expelled from the college and was then remanded by the court into the care of his horrified parents.

A day after his parents had brought Curt home, their car stuffed with all of his college possessions, Nikki called me with the mind-numbing news. Over the course of the next several months, I visited at length with Curt, as well as with his parents. Predictably those conversations were shot through with sorrow, shame, bitterness, betrayal. They were unlike any others I had ever experienced.

Then came the call with the special request. Nikki, sobbing on the other end of the line, said they had just been notified by Curt's attorney he was to appear before the judge in twenty days. At that time, with a plea bargain having been negotiated by his attorney, he would be formally sentenced to forty-five to sixty months in the state penitentiary system. He was to present himself with just the clothes on his back. Nothing else. At the close of the court appearance he would be handcuffed and led directly from the court to begin serving his sentence.

Knowing what lay in store for Curt and his family on that day, Nikki now explained to me over the phone that she and Herb, her grieving husband, would be profoundly grateful if I drove the family to and from the court hearing. "There's no way," she understandably noted, "that Herb or I could drive."

"Of course," I immediately answered. "Of course." I didn't know what else to say. There was silence on both ends. Not the kind of silence that is born in shy uncertainty, but silence that betrays a depth of pain beyond words. I hung up a few moments later and then sat at my desk, in a fog. "Lord," I mumbled, "what have I gotten myself into?" Well, I knew the simple answer to that question. It was all that came *with* that simple answer that was giving me pause.

The next nineteen days passed all too quickly. For me, yes, but especially for Curt and his family. Early on day twenty, I drove into their driveway. Within seconds the front door opened and out stumbled Nikki, Nikki's sister, Herb, and their daughter. I embraced each, sensing the profound grief that gripped them. Nikki choked, "He'll be right out. He wanted a couple of minutes alone in his bedroom." Five minutes later Curt joined us. Herb sat stiff backed in the front seat, staring straight ahead. Nikki and her sister were squeezed shoulder to shoulder, hand in hand, in the middle seat of the minivan. Curt stooped into the vehicle, pulled the door closed behind himself, nodded ever so slightly at me with a downcast expression, and then slid into the far back seat beside his stone-faced sister.

Awkwardly I asked no one in particular, "Shall we go?" I saw Nikki nod her head in the rear view mirror. Herb looked straight ahead without glancing in my direction. Curt, his head visible in the mirror between those of his mother and aunt, was red-eyed. His lips were tight, yet betrayed a quiver.

We then drove in silence for one hundred and forty miles, without stopping. It was the saddest drive of my life, bar none. It surpassed even the mournful treks to the cemeteries where I was witness to the interments of my parents, grandparents, and dear friends. Words seemed unnecessary, almost offensive.

On arrival at the court we quietly emptied out of the vehicle. After a moment of orienting ourselves, we followed the signs that directed us into the right building. We single-filed through the mandatory security check, a blank-faced clerk signing everyone in. She then led us silently into the small courtroom. A bailiff directed us to the hard chairs behind the bar. Reading from a clipboard, he brusquely called out Curt's name. When Curt stood, the bailiff wordlessly pointed to a seat immediately in front of the judge's bench. Realizing what the moment represented, Curt stood and hugged his mother. Then his father. Then his sister and aunt. And then his mother one last time.

Once Curt was seated up front, we waited in silence for several minutes. In through the main door came Curt's attorney. He nodded in our direction and sat down next to Curt. The judge entered from a side door, looking at no one. He took his seat. He looked up, straight at Curt. He addressed him by his full name and instructed him to rise. Curt, along with his attorney, stood. His face was a mask of grief. He answered the judge's questions and listened silently as the judge reviewed the plea agreement and the sentence. The judge proceeded to note how Curt had not only irreparably wounded the victim's sense of wellbeing, but had besmirched the names of his fellow Eagle Scouts. Curt listened and nodded. When the judge asked him if he had anything to say, Curt said quietly he was profoundly sorry for what he had done. He had no excuses, he said. He was ready to serve his time. With that, the judge instructed the officer standing nearby to handcuff Curt and to remand him to the jail until a prison assignment was arranged by the state.

Watching and listening, I was aware I was in as dark a place, emotionally and spiritually, as I had ever been. Mute, along with each of Curt's loved ones, I barely breathed as I witnessed his handcuffing and subsequent removal from court. Curt never turned around nor said a word over his shoulder. Nikki, sobbing, cried, "We love you, Curt."

Then he was gone.

The judge left the room. The bailiff nodded at us and pointed to the door. That was it. We rose, gave one another hugs, and then departed.

The drive home felt immeasurably heavy, even more so than the drive to the court. For stretches all five of us remained silent. I concentrated on the road. Nikki and her sister quietly consoled each other, while Curt's sister sat numbly speechless, alone in the rear seat. Up front Herb stared straight ahead, much as he had done earlier. Every fifteen minutes I found myself reaching over with my right hand, squeezing his left leg gently. Each time, somewhat to my amazement, his left hand covered mine and gave me a squeeze back.

Finally, half an hour from home Herb spoke. "Thank you, Bob." Though he didn't turn his head to look at me, the tremble in his voice was profoundly moving.

"You're more than welcome, Herb." That was all. But that was enough. For someone prone to gab and chatter, it was for me in so many ways one of countless learning moments, not the least of which came in recognizing we humans are fashioned in mysteriously wonderful ways. While it behooves us regularly to be clear in our discourse, it all the more matters we allow our presence to say what our words cannot.

Three years and nine months later, I knocked at their front door. I could hear undeniable evidence from within that a family was letting loose, soaking up the relief and joy.

The door flew open. Standing there was Nikki, a new grandchild hanging on her hip. As I stepped into the living room, she threw her free arm around me. She led me into the kitchen, where a small crowd was gathered. As we entered Curt rose from his chair, walked in our direction, and met me halfway. We embraced. Hard. Wordlessly.

Smiling, with tears coursing down her cheeks, Nikki said, "Pastor Bob, allow me to introduce you to Uncle Curt."

36

I'm a Visitor

Typically the greeters would smile and say, "Welcome." They would then step aside to let me find my own way to a pew. All too rarely would anyone then do more than look at me, sometimes with a slight nod of the head if I happened to catch them glancing in my direction during the subsequent worship service. Following the benediction, I often would end up departing the sanctuary with barely a word spoken to me.

For several years I had wondered what it would be like to be a visitor walking into a new church building on an ordinary Sunday. I wondered because of what I had begun to see much too frequently while standing at the door of my own congregation's sanctuary at the close of many services. On those fairly frequent occasions when one or more visitors had been our guests for worship, I would oftentimes notice them after the benediction, standing in the line in order to greet me. They would stand in that line, with some folks in front of them waiting to say "hi" to me, and with some other folks standing behind them, as well. More often than not—very much more often than not, quite sadly—no one would be speaking with the visitors. Those instances would irk me, if not indeed anger me. Once the visitors would ultimately stand directly before me in order to exchange greetings, I would then grab those still standing behind them and introduce everyone to one another. Gratefully, once introduced to one another, conversation would unfold, sometimes at short length, and sometimes at greater length.

But that being said, it never ceased to alarm me to see visitors in our midst essentially ignored—this within and by a congregation that insistently self-identified as being "warm and friendly."

Then came my first sabbatical from regular pastoral responsibilities. For two months I was set free each Sunday to worship with other congregations. That's when I decided, with curiosity-laden intentionality, to play—well, to be—a visitor. I wanted to experience what visitors in my own congregation experienced. To that end I visited a different congregation on eight successive Sundays. Every Sunday I would enter the main door of a new church building some five or ten minutes before the service commenced. I would shake the hand of those posted at the door as greeters, and I would say, "Hi. My name's Bob. I'm a visitor." This was my way of saying, "Hi. I'm a potential new member. You know, new member, like what you and your fellow congregants moan about needing more of."

In almost all eight of those instances the greeters would smile and say, "Welcome." They would then step aside to let me find my own way to a pew. All too rarely would anyone then do more than look at me, sometimes with a slight nod of the head if I happened to catch them glancing in my direction during the subsequent worship service. Following the benediction, often I would end up departing the sanctuary with hardly a word spoken to me. In fact, I would fairly regularly wander to the back of the sanctuary, stand in line with others waiting to greet the pastor, and find that no one— *no* one—would talk to me, even when I would try to initiate conversation with those in front or behind me in the line. Typically those folks would be talking amongst themselves, likely reconnecting with friends whom they hadn't seen in seven days or more. When I would finally arrive at the spot occupied by the glad-handing pastor, I would again say, "Hi. My name's Bob. I'm a visitor." Typically the pastor would indicate it was good to have me present. "Do come back, Bob" was the norm. On several of those Sundays I had located a card to fill out with my contact information. They were typically in the pew racks, alongside of the hymnbooks. I would fill them out and place them in the offering plate, per their instruction. On less than half of those instances did I subsequently hear from the congregation.

That eight week pilgrimage through the wilderness of congregations like my own—congregations who in all likelihood also insistently self-identified as "warm and friendly"—was a lonely enterprise. To say it was illuminating, in a distressing sense, would be understatement. By the fourth or fifth week of the eight, I decided to act. On the subsequent Monday mornings I intentionally and carefully wrote personal notes to the pastor of the church visited the day before. After expressing appropriate words of thanks for the opportunity to worship as a guest with her or his parishioners, I then described my experience of being, for all practical purposes, ignored during my visit.

What was illuminating was what I heard back from practically every one of those pastors. Most expressed their surprise, as well as compassionate regret, that I had experienced isolation rather than reception during my visit. Two of them asked my permission for them to share my personal note with their governing boards, indicating they had been trying valiantly to lift up for their well-meaning parishioners how their impression of themselves being "warm and friendly" fell short of the reality experienced by at least one, if not many, of their many Sunday morning visitors.

Upon returning to my full pastoral duties at the conclusion of that sabbatical, I determined to share in bold detail my fairly lonely experience as a visitor of other church communities during the previous weeks. I invited my beloved parishioners to join me in honestly examining how, even *if*, we were indeed being truly and regularly embracing of visitors in our midst. In response, a significant number of the membership covenanted to be more intentional about spotting, welcoming, and engaging visitors. What several honestly shared with me over the subsequent months was they realized that covenanting came with a price. They described how finding and conversing with visitors deprived them of precious time for reconnecting with their own congregational friends, including those whom they rarely had the opportunity to see between Sundays. They also noted that sacrifice was worthwhile, albeit somewhat painful. One even suggested naming their changed behavior as sacrificial, indicating assertively talking with visitors was a significant faith-step. She acknowledged losing a little catch-up time with a dear friend, in favor of extending herself to a visitor, brought to mind for her what some of the costliness of Christian discipleship may well entail.

I suspect that dear ol' Dietrich Bonhoeffer, who wrote so eloquently about the various costs of discipleship, would have wholeheartedly agreed with her.

37

Sacred Secrecy

"AND THE ONLY ONES who will be present, or even know about it, will be Mom and Dad."

I probably blinked as I listened to Lou Anne's request, including this caveat about secrecy. It was a first for me. I had never before been asked to officiate at a wedding where only four individuals would know about it.

Lou Anne was the daughter of family friends in a nearby town. I had known her family since she was in grade school. Since then she had progressed all the way through graduate school where she had met John, a computer whiz. They had dated and ultimately were engaged. Now employed by the state, John was also in the Army Reserves. When Lou Anne had earlier introduced John to me, they noted it was likely he would be called up to active duty and deployed to Iraq at some point in the near future. While still mulling over as a twosome when and how to plan for a full wedding, John got the word. He would be shipping out in two weeks and would likely not be back stateside for at least six to twelve months.

That's when Lou Anne called me. They came to my study that evening, hand in hand and red-eyed. I invited them to sit on the couch in my study, which they did, shoulder to shoulder at first, but then with John's arm wrapped protectively around Lou Anne. They quietly told me they had spent all afternoon discussing the options. "We've decided not to wait to be married, Pastor Bob," said Lou Anne. Looking at her fiancé, she said, "We want to be married this weekend, before John leaves for the base."

"Okay," I responded slowly. "Where and when are you thinking about for the service?" I was already reaching for the calendar on my desk, trying to recall what if anything may already have been scheduled for the sanctuary that Saturday.

"Well," said John when Lou Anne kept looking at him rather than at me. "We've decided to have the wedding service here. In your study. This Saturday afternoon, if that would work for you."

Not anticipating those details, I simply nodded. Before I managed to say anything, Lou Anne picked up John's train of thought. "And the only ones who will be present, or even know about it, will be Mom and Dad."

That's when I likely blinked, as I tried to process what I had just heard. They awaited my response, looking at me with a sad but focused determination in their eyes. "Okay," I said again. "Let's work this one through a bit. Help me to understand better what you're thinking." Which is exactly what they did.

It was John, normally the far more subdued of the two, who explained. "We still want to have a full, proper wedding, with all of our family and friends in attendance, but we intend to have it only when I'm back from Iraq." He stopped, looking Lou Anne in the eye. Then, looking back at me, he continued. "But I want Lou Anne to be my wife, legally, before I'm deployed." He stopped. Then he said, "Just in case. Because you never know."

Oh.

That's when I found my own eyes misting a bit, as well. Not as much as theirs already were, but moving in that direction.

John continued. "So our idea, Reverend, is to have a private service, with license and everything, right here in your study this Saturday afternoon. That'll make it official, and I can then give my commanding officer the required paper work." I nodded, listening. "That way Lou Anne will get all the benefits, even if I don't make it back." As he stopped, his face remained stock still. Lou Anne's began to crumble, with lips quivering.

"I see." Then to both of them I asked, "And you'd like Lou Anne's parents to be present, but not yours, John?"

"That's correct, sir." Now looking down at his feet, he continued. "They don't need to know, and I'm not sure how they'd handle it. Not because of Lou Anne. They love her. They can't wait for us to be married." I waited for him to continue. "It's just that, if they know we're getting married because, you know, of what might happen to me, I'm not sure if they'd handle that so well." I waited. "I don't want to give them any more reason to worry than they'll already have."

That's when Lou Anne's damp face began to shine with pride, with compassion, with a wife's love.

"How about your parents, Lou Anne? You want them here?"

"Absolutely, Pastor Bob. We've already talked it through with them, and they understand completely." She looked at her fiancé's face, now revealing a streak of tears flowing from each eye. To me she said, "We both want family with us when we exchange our vows, but Mom and Dad are the only ones that make sense to us now under these circumstances."

I nodded and then wiped my own tears. "I'd be honored." They both looked at me, gently smiling and quietly sobbing at the same time.

That Saturday, robed on their request, I stood before them and Lou Anne's parents. As they exchanged their wedding vows, it hit me. When all is said and done, this, *this* is what a wedding is all about. Stripped of all the delightful, customary accoutrements—the flowers, the pageantry, the apparel—as much as those have their place and add to the moment, the essence of that moment is found in the pledging of unconditional love and fidelity between two bared souls, witnessed by those who will compassionately support those souls on behalf of the one who brought them together in the first place.

That wedding in my study? It was the most meaningful of any I've ever been privileged to officiate. There were tears. There were embraces. There were pledges that would stand the test of time.

And then a year later the same vows were exchanged again, with more than a hundred relatives and friends in attendance, exulting in the unabashed affection on display as John and Lou Anne made fully public what God had already done with and for them twelve months earlier.

38

Down to Earth

THE DOZEN OR SO adolescents stared at Juliana. None said a word. None looked as though they had a speck of interest in her question. But not to be rebuffed by a group of young teens, she asked again, "No really. What do you think heaven will look like?"

One or two of the youth stirred, maybe feeling a bit of guilt that they weren't responding to their typically appreciated youth advisor. One of them was Juliana's daughter Ginger, who had familial motivation to try, if at all possible, to respond to her mother's otherwise embarrassment-inducing query. In an effort to quell Juliana's eagerness—or was it frustration?—Ginger suggested, "I guess full of clouds and stuff." A couple of her teen friends giggled quietly. "Yeah, clouds. But with everyone floating around, kinda."

Ginger's mother nodded, acknowledging her daughter's valiant attempt to get things rolling. But she said nothing, until again, "What do you think heaven will look like? You know, in addition to clouds."

Now not even Ginger was going to rescue her mother. Silence reigned supreme, until I heard myself say, "Maybe we could tackle that question by looking at a passage in Revelation." Juliana nodded vigorously in my direction, clearly desperate for the life preserver I was tossing her way.

133

I was sitting as a guest in the circle. It was Friday evening, youth group night. I was there as a fill-in for our youth ministry staff person who was on vacation. Prior to leaving town he had met with Juliana and provided her with the evening's topical material, including an exploration of what heaven is, and will be, all about. The staff person had asked me to attend in his place, providing back-up support to Juliana, if need be.

Support was well needed, I now realized.

The teens shifted their gaze from Juliana to me. Their expressions didn't reveal much more interest in my suggestion than had been the case with Juliana's opening question. "But there's not much to be lost by forging ahead," I thought to myself. So I said, "In the Bible there are a variety of pictures that are painted about heaven, but the one I've always found most intriguing is from the last book in the Bible."

The kids stared mutely at me.

I continued. "In that book it's suggested there will be a day coming in the future when Jesus will return to be here with us. Here, on earth, where we already live."

They continued to stare at me.

"The writer of Revelation then goes on to suggest heaven will come down here. To earth." A flicker of interest, if not bemusement, on a couple of faces. "The idea is that where we live isn't going to disappear, or be wiped out, or whatever. It's going to remain. And with good reason! It's a beautiful world God has made and allowed us to live in. God doesn't want to destroy it, but to renew it. Make it fresh, the way God first made it."

"Oh, you mean like the Garden of Eden?" The question came from an unexpected source. Ralph was one of the quieter members of the youth group, albeit one who seemed to have the respect of most of the other kids.

"Yeah, that's right!" I responded with delight. "Revelation paints a picture of heaven coming down to earth and making earth be like that first Garden, where everything and everyone lived in harmony."

Remarkably a few of the teens began to stir. Their body language betrayed some curiosity. "So things will look the same, but kinda different?" intoned Nora, one of the bolder members of the circle.

"Exactly!" I exclaimed. "The same, but very different!"

"So no clouds?" asked Ginger. Several in the circle laughed.

"Well, clouds when it needs to rain, I suppose," I responded. "But not clouds to float around in, I suspect." Now they were all staring at me, but no longer bored. Now their eyes suggested intrigue, if not confusion. I glanced at Juliana. Her expression invited—well, screamed for—me to proceed. The floor was mine. "Okay. Let's go with this idea for a few minutes." A dozen or more pairs of eyes stared at me. "If indeed heaven will come down here, to earth, what do you think might be the result? What kinds of things do you think God might do with the way things are here?"

Silence, until Bart said, "Maybe he'll open the jails?"

"Say more about that, Bart."

"Maybe God will let all the prisoners out, and then he'll do something else with the jails."

"Go on. Or anyone else want to join in?"

"Yeah, maybe he'll change the jails," suggested Crystal. I nodded, and she continued. "If it's heaven, then there won't be any need for jails. Maybe God will change the jails into housing for homeless people?"

"Whoa," I thought to myself. Before I had a chance to react aloud, several heads began to nod. Smiles began to show themselves around the circle. Then a chorus of reactions: "Yeah! Everyone will have a place to live!" "And hospitals! We won't need hospitals, because sick people won't be sick anymore, right?" Vigorous nodding. "Maybe God will make hospitals into museums." "Or into schools!" "Or maybe into places where old people can go to have neighbors!" "But will there be old people in heaven?" "Hadn't thought about that!"

I sat there, along with Juliana, who glanced in my direction. We smiled briefly at each other, overwhelmed by what had just begun to happen. The youth proceeded to explore the mystery of what lies not just ahead, but around. They began to list aloud all the places around the globe that will be readied for transformation once heaven descends upon our beloved planet. Military bases were pictured as being made into amusement parks. Landfills became excavation sites of unimaginably exciting discoveries of old things made new. And most amazing of all, the group began to list the good things, like youth groups, that won't disappear to be replaced but will be renewed for everyone to enjoy.

The imagining was unbounded. The envisioning was astonishing.

By the end of the evening the youth continued to chatter as they moved to the parking lot where their parents awaited them. The energy unleashed somehow lingered in the air, even after the cars had all driven off. I stood in the empty lot, staring upward, not at the steeple nearby, but at the stars and beyond.

"Whoa," I found myself thinking again. "Whoa."

39

Choosing Rightly

He blinked at me, understandably not sure how to answer.

"No, seriously, Timothy. Are you familiar with *The Price is Right*?"

He blinked again and then said, "Yeah, I guess, Pastor Bob. I've seen it sometimes. But what does that have to do with my trying to figure out what God wants me to do with my life?"

I smiled. "Well, let me explain by telling you a personal story." Then, in response to Timothy's having come to seek pastoral guidance about how to discern what vocational path to take moving from undergraduate life into the workplace, I told him about Bob Barker and *The Price is Right*.

✳ ✳ ✳

It was mid-August during the summer between my junior and senior years in college. I was heading back to campus in the next couple of weeks, planning to finish my studies with dual majors in math and philosophy, knowing those majors didn't carry with them much guarantee of employment upon graduation. I had been giving serious consideration to three options for post-college pursuits. One was to head to seminary. Another was to head to graduate school. And the third was to opt out of the school track, and to head over to the Middle East for a year of volunteer work. Each of the options was both mildly appealing and somewhat daunting.

By early August of that summer I was churning within. My father, along with my mother, could tell. So, as was Dad's routine on occasional Sunday afternoons, he invited me to join him for a walk around town. Some five minutes into our pedestrian outing, he said, "You seem to be troubled a bit these days."

I shot him a sideways glance, nodded, and said, "You can tell?"

"Yup. What's up?" After a bit of silence, measuring what to say, I explained to my beloved father how I was tied up in knots, trying to figure out what God wanted me to do next year after graduation. On his invitation, I explained how I had three scenarios I was currently considering, but didn't know which was the "right" one to pursue. "How so?" he asked.

"Well, I want to do what God wants me to do. But I'm not sure which of those three paths is the one God wants for me."

We kept walking as he remained silent for five, maybe ten seconds. He then said, "Sounds like you think God is like Bob Barker."

"Excuse me?"

"Sounds like you picture God being like Bob Barker. You know—the host of *The Price is Right*."

I was speechless, if for no reason other than I had no clue Dad knew about Bob Barker and his zany game show. And what on earth was his point? I responded, not hiding my amusement and confusion, "Yeah, I know about Bob Barker and his show." Still walking together, I continued. "But I didn't know you knew about him." He smiled, but gave no explanation. So I then stopped walking, as did he. I turned to him as we stood on the sidewalk, and asked, "What on earth do you mean I'm picturing God being like crazy Bob Barker?"

He continued to grin, turned, and began to walk. Not wanting to be left behind, in every sense of the expression, I also turned and caught up with him. "Well," he said, "listening to you it sounds like you've got three really wonderful options to choose from next year. It also sounds like you're picturing those options as being behind three doors, sort of like on *The Price is Right*. And it also sounds like you think you're supposed to know which of the doors is the one God wants you to choose, but God won't let you know ahead of time which one it is. It's as though God's a little bit like Bob Barker with his contestants: better guess right, or you're gonna end up with the booby prize."

As we walked, he fell silent, allowing me to mull over this odd analogy.

"It seems as though some of your anxiety, Bob, comes from presuming that what matters is guessing—okay, we'll call it discerning—what God's will is for you, and that God is teasing you with three intriguing doors, when only one is the right one, and that God is behind only that one right door."

"Okay," I said slowly, still unsure where Dad was going with all of this.

"How about thinking about those doors in a more biblical way?"

"What do you mean?"

"What scripture makes pretty clear is that God never, ever abandons us. Even, maybe *especially*, when we make choices, including poor ones." We stopped, and he looked me in the eye. "Behind all three of your doors is God. God's not behind just 'the right' one." We started walking again. He continued, "It really helps me to know that when I'm having to choose between good options, God's going to be there, on the other side of the door, so to speak, no matter which choice I make from among those good options."

"Go on."

"What matters to God, Bob, is that we choose rightly. Not that we make the right choice. It's that we make good choices the right way: trusting God will be with us, no matter what."

"Hmm," I thought to myself. "What matters is trust. That God is Emmanuel—God *with* us."

By the time we had wandered back to our house, I realized the knot in my stomach had begun to loosen. That the immobilizing anxiety was, well, lessening its grip on me because I had three really good options from which to choose. To choose rightly. To choose with trust.

✳ ✳ ✳

I looked at Timothy. He was looking back at me, now with a hint of a grin. "So, Pastor Bob, all I need to do—no, *can* do—is trust God to be there no matter what I choose to do?"

"And then when you take your next step—"

"—it'll be a leap of faith—of trust!" Timothy's eyes lit up in recognition.

Some time later I thought for sure, as Timothy was leaving my study and heading to his car, I could heard him chuckle, saying "Wait till I tell Mom and Dad that God's not like Bob Barker!"

40

My God, my God

I FELT HEARTBROKEN FOR Gregory. I felt powerless to do anything. I realized though, when all was said, there was nothing to be done.

Gregory and I knew each other very well. A decade earlier he and his late wife had been instrumental in welcoming my family when we had moved into the parsonage. He and I had had many interactions, some during committee meetings, some on the softball field, and many at the time of his wife's passing a few years earlier. Gregory had been retired for some time but had been blessed with stable health until just the past few months. Then he began to display symptoms which raised alarms. His primary care physician ultimately referred him to an oncologist, and he was now in that doctor's care.

Cancer was eating away at his skeletal system, as frequently happens with late stage metastases. Even when he tried to lie perfectly still, the pain had become distressing, if not excruciating. He had been admitted to the ICU three days earlier, with the goal of his medical team trying in every manner possible to reduce, if not eliminate, that pain. Regrettably, their efforts were proving less than successful.

As I had done the previous two days, I was now standing bedside in the ICU cubicle, looking Gregory in the eye. With beeping monitors, IV drips, and a plethora of other medical paraphernalia encircling his bed, Gregory's facial expression betrayed anxiety, if not terror. He stared straight up at the ceiling, with only occasional sideway glances in my direction. Teeth gritted, he finally moaned, "I can't take it, Bob. I can't take it."

I nodded. "I understand, Gregory. I can tell."

For ten, maybe twenty seconds, he repeated his desperation. "I can't. I can't take it."

"I know, Gregory."

Finally, with a look that truly sent chills down my spine, he looked at me and growled—yes, growled. "Unplug me. Now."

"Unplug you, Gregory?"

"Pull the damn plug. Now."

"What plug?"

"Whatever plug's keeping me alive." He looked back and forth at the machines and lines to his right and left. "Find whatever's keeping me alive and unplug it." He closed his eyes and then opened them again, looking me directly in the eye. With palpable anger he declared, "I want to die. Now. And I can't do it by myself. *You* have to do it." I stared at him, paralyzed. "Do it!" he grunted, grimacing in pain. In fury, his voice shook, "*Do it!*"

I glanced out the entryway of his cubicle, hoping that someone—anyone wearing medical garb—might hear him and come into the cubicle. No one heard him. No one came. There I stood, not moving. Now far more softly, with eyes closed, he repeated, "Do it. I can't take this anymore."

I felt heartbroken for Gregory. I felt powerless to do anything, and I realized that, when all was said, there was nothing to be done.

"I understand, Gregory. I truly do." He opened his eyes and looked pleadingly at me. I continued, "I wish I could, but I can't. You know I can't. That's not for me to do." In retrospect, I confess I actually expected him to agree with me. I somehow anticipated he would nod quietly, soberly, and respond with "You're right, I know."

That expectation couldn't have been more misguided.

Rather than understanding my existential and ethical quandary, Gregory glared at me. "Yes, it is. It *is* for you to do. Pull the plug. Do whatever it takes. I'm done, and you're the one who's going to make it happen." The ferocity in his voice was both numbing and agitating. I stood stock-still, absolutely bereft of any idea of what to say or do.

After as tense a few seconds of silence as I'd ever known, I responded, "Gregory, it's not for me to do. It's not for anyone to do. I'm sorry. I feel deeply pained that you hurt so much. I understand you want the pain to be over. I really do. The doctors are doing whatever they can to make that happen. All I can do is to ask God to relieve your pain and to help you through this hard time."

Before I continued my well-intentioned, platitude-filled response, he interrupted. "Then get out. Get out!" He turned to face the far side of the cubicle. "Get out. Now." I was speechless. As much as I hurt for him, I realized I was hurting for myself, as selfish a feeling as that was. "Get out. Now," he repeated.

"As you wish, Gregory." I quietly left the cubicle, heading to the nurses' station. I found his charge nurse and described to her what Gregory's pain level seemed to be. She noted, with not much more than a shrug, all of the staff well knew his pain level, and they were doing all they could for him. With that she turned and walked away. I stood, alone in the wash of white coats and green scrubs moving around me. I felt empty, stripped of all the trappings of my pastoral role. Stripped even of any illusion of ability to effect change and be a supportive presence to my agonized neighbor.

Later that afternoon I crumbled into the desk chair back in my study. I felt empty. I mumbled a prayer on Gregory's behalf and another on my own. Both were intoned in quiet, but also with a grimace that somehow mirrored the one on Gregory's face earlier that day in his cubicle.

That's when I looked up and saw, for the first time in a long while, the small cross I had hung years earlier on the wall facing my desk. I stared at it. I swear, even today, I then heard a faint whisper from that six-inch piece of olive wood. The whisper queried in agony, "My God, my God, why have you forsaken me?" (Matthew 27:46)

I could not rip my gaze from the cross. Nor could I ignore those words, cried out in insufferable pain by one—maybe the *only* one—who could be with Gregory in his.

The next morning I returned to the ICU. On arrival I found an orderly straightening out Gregory's now empty cubicle. He informed me in a matter of fact way "the patient" had died the previous hour. I watched the orderly for a moment or two, and then quietly departed. As I walked down corridor and stairwell, and then out the exit ramp to the hospital's expansive garage, I silently offered thanks. I confessed to the one who had cried from the cross that I was grateful beyond measure Gregory was now whole—and wholly his.

41

Family of God

OUR DAUGHTER WAS SITTING on the couch beside her husband, holding in her arms their less than one week old daughter, Katherine. Emily and Matt were displaying that incomparable gaze of first time parents, while Mary and I were doing the same from a few feet away as first time grandparents.

A memory, a feeling, welled up within me. Looking at the three of them together on the couch felt the same but different. Maybe more to the point, it felt the same but broader. I found myself recalling the first time I had held Emily nearly three decades earlier, shortly after her own birth. I began to realize that experience was both emotionally identical to, and yet symbolically broadened by, this moment of witnessing the birth of a new family.

I vividly remember being overwhelmed the first time I had held our newborn daughter in my arms. I had looked back and forth between her and my wife. I couldn't get enough of looking at each of those two amazing gifts God had given to me. I recall discovering in that hospital room so long ago that with Emily's birth something new was happening to me. In contrast to the way I had fallen deeply in love with Mary over the course of many months as we had come to know each other years earlier, I now was in love virtually instantaneously. Looking into infant Emily's eyes I realized I loved her. Immediately. Unquestioningly. She was my daughter and I was her parent. Already I loved her, even though I hardly knew her, whatever it meant even to use such words to describe an infant just learning how to breathe on her own.

Holding Emily in my arms, I knew I loved her. In that knowledge was born a certainty, equally immediate and unquestioning, that such was the love of the God of all creation for each and every one of the divine one's children. If I so loved my child, so too did, and does, our maker love every single one of the human family. Moreover I realized just as my parental commitment was forever established in that first face to face meeting with my daughter, so too is the eternal one's commitment for me and every one of our sisters and brothers who will ever stir within our mothers' wombs.

Emily's arrival gave birth to my unabashed conviction that God's primal love for every creature is not a choice, but a given.

Now watching Emily, Matt, and their own days-old daughter, something not yet explored began to take shape. Looking at the three of them together on their couch felt the same but different. It felt the same but broader. It felt the same in that I once again found myself loving whom I was seeing. But now that "whom" was not an individual. It was a family. A new family. A family of two generations, not just one. A family not just by chance, but by design. By their designer. I realized in that moment that my love was now not only for each of the three, but for all of the three. I was in love with this new family. My love felt the same but different. It felt the same but broader.

That's when it hit me. We—all of us, bar none—are the one family of our maker, and are loved as a *family*, just as much as we are each loved as individuals.

In that moment the biblical stories—the biblical *story*—made so much more sense. Our God has been, and continues to be, in the family-building business. As deep as her divine love is for each child, so deep as well is his divine love for each family. Just as the eternal one has parental affection for each newborn, even more broadly does that one embrace and bless each new family—or even more mysteriously, the one family of all creation, from those that swim in the deep, to those that sow on the plain and soar through the air.

The Sunday morning after first meeting Emily, Matt, and Katherine as a new family, I stepped into the pulpit and was overwhelmed by what I truly began to see for the first time: not just a collection of beloved individuals, but one family of multiple generations, fashioned and celebrated by the gracious heart of the one who loves each, but who just as much loves all.

42

Cross Values

I REALIZED ALMOST INSTANTANEOUSLY Gail expected me to affirm, if not applaud, her decisive pronouncement. But I couldn't. And I wouldn't, as counterintuitive as that decision may have felt to both Gail and me.

Gail and her fiancé, Jerome, were sitting side by side on the couch in my study. I sat facing them, with their pre-marriage questionnaire results in my lap. They had approached me several weeks earlier that fall about officiating at their wedding, scheduled for the following summer. Gail I already knew, as she had grown up in the congregation I served, though had long ago become uninvolved during college, graduate school, and her early career years in the area.

We had already met as a threesome for three full sessions, each two hours in length. We had done some preliminary overview of their wedding plans, and then they had each shared a detailed summary of their life stories, from childhood through adolescence, college, and graduate studies, and concluding with how they had met and become engaged.

I liked Gail and Jerome very much. They were very forthcoming with each other and with me, allowing us to do some significant exploration of a host of issues surrounding their impending entry into married life. With the arrival of this fourth session, we were beginning to dive into the area of religious expectations that each was bringing into their relationship. In reviewing their responses in the questionnaire, I had noted to myself that Jerome had answered the pertinent questions with clear, unabashed honesty that he would not be participating in the life of any church congregation in the decades ahead. Gail, on the other hand, answered the same questions with a definitive assertion that she intended for her entire family—both parents and any and all forthcoming offspring—to attend church on a regular basis.

Their definitive disclosures begged to be highlighted and addressed. To that end I said, "Jerome, when you filled out and swapped each other's questionnaire responses, I'm sure you noted that your intent not to be active in a congregation stands in contrast to Gail's intent to have your whole family be active. Thoughts?"

Looking first at me, and then directly at Gail beside him, he responded, "I feel personally no need to be part of a church. Sundays are full of other things I'm accustomed to doing. But I'll have no problem with Gail attending church and taking our children with her."

I nodded, saying, "I appreciate your honesty." Turning to Gail I asked her, "Your thoughts?"

Gail smiled at me, then at Jerome. "Oh, don't worry, Pastor Bob. I'll get him to come with me. It'll just be a matter of time before he changes his mind about coming."

Jerome stared pleasantly at his fiancée and then looked at me. "Won't happen, Pastor Bob."

"Oh, he'll come around," intoned Gail immediately, looking at me with an expression that suggested I could take her assurance to the bank.

I realized almost instantaneously Gail expected me to affirm, if not applaud, her decisive pronouncement. But I couldn't. And I wouldn't, as counterintuitive as that decision may have felt to both Gail and me. "Are you hearing what he's saying in apparently full and honest disclosure, Gail?"

"Oh, I hear him alright." Then again looking sideways at Jerome, she said, "But he'll come around."

To Jerome I said, "I appreciate your honesty, Jerome." And to Gail I said, "I'm feeling some discomfort about your stated plan to change Jerome when he's being honest about his intents." She stared at me, saying nothing. "One's spiritual life, I believe, is rooted in what one values. It seems to me that Jerome is making it clear his values do not include church participation. I'm hearing you indicate you intend to change his values."

"Well, I expect he will change. I'll make it happen."

"I'm not sure how you think you'll be able to make it happen, Gail." Then looking at each of them in turn, I continued, "One thing that life has begun to teach me over the years is that I'm not able to change anyone else, especially when it comes to their values." Their smiles had disappeared at this point, as I then said, "Short of pointing a gun at someone and forcing him or her to do something under duress, I know of no way to make someone do what I want them to. Especially when it comes to what they sincerely believe."

Silence.

"Jerome, I'm hearing you say your values do not include participation in a church."

"That's right, Pastor Bob."

"Gail, I'm hearing you say your values do include participation in a church." She nodded. "And I'm hearing you say your values are that that participation should be by your whole family, including the father of your future children." She nodded again. "Well, in all honesty, I question whether you'll be able to make that happen. If you believe you can shape Jerome, changing the way he values or doesn't value church life, I'm concerned that you're setting yourself up for disappointment and frustration, and setting Jerome up for feeling manipulated or even of being disrespected."

Jerome now nodded. Gail stared at me, then at the floor. She then looked at her fiancé and said, "I'll make it happen. You watch."

I looked directly at Jerome, saying nothing. He in turn looked at me, then at Gail, and then back at me. He smiled and said, "Won't happen."

The impasse, if not the fundamental unwillingness to recognize the concern I was attempting to lift up for both them, was jarring to me. I stated so. In response, remarkably, each said to me, "Don't worry, Pastor Bob. We'll be fine."

The following summer they exchanged vows before me and their extended circles of family and friends. They did so in the sanctuary in which Gail had been raised.

Three years later Gail gave birth to their first child. I had not seen them in the interim. A month after the child's arrival Gail phoned and asked me if I would please baptize their infant daughter. I did so during a subsequent service, hearing her, with her silent husband standing beside her, promise to raise her child in the life of the church.

I did not see any of them in the sanctuary for two more years, with the exception of Christmas Eve. Then, second verse, same as the first. Child number two, a son, was born. A second baptism was requested. The baptism unfolded, with more promises made by Gail.

I did not see any of them in the sanctuary for the next several years, with the exception of Christmas Eve.

I then retired, leaving town, as well as leaving the family of four behind. As best I could tell, the marriage was relatively strong. As best I could tell, Jerome's values had remained intact. Gail had not managed to change them.

I've wondered, however. I've wondered whether Jerome's unchanged values had quietly impacted Gail's own. Could it be that his values, honestly professed from day one and honored by his unchanged behavior on virtually every Sunday morning, had slowly changed—even corroded—hers? Why else would she have ignored, for all practical purposes, the promises she had made—not to me in my study, but to the one in whose presence she had brought both of her children for baptism?

43

To Such as These

It was one of the more unscripted, soul-stirring moments I'd ever experienced.

Or so I thought.

A little earlier, as I had listened to the organ prelude, I glanced around the sanctuary to see who was in attendance. I noticed Melinda had invited a fellow third grader to worship with her and her mother. Melinda was a sweetie—a cheery, bright girl who clearly had a warm heart for her peers. That Sunday morning she and her mother, Anna, had brought with them to be a guest in worship one of Melinda's closest companions from school, Brandi.

Brandi was an exceptional child. Born almost totally deaf, as well as with severely impaired vision, she was raised by extraordinary parents. Not unlike Helen Keller, Brandi was not going to be held back by her disabilities. Mainstreamed in public school, with a fulltime aide who signed for her throughout each school day, she was proving to be an outstanding student. Brandi and Melinda had become fast friends from kindergarten on, with the wonderful result that Melinda had learned to sign with striking efficiency.

I well recall seeing the two girls, who were classmates of our son, again and again engaged in intense conversation in their classroom, the school cafeteria, wherever. Those conversations were fascinating to behold as they unfolded in silence with the girls' faces no more than twelve inches apart, their four hands signing to each other at an almost frenzied pace. Their expressions would veer from smiles to frowns, from surprise to anger. You name it, they displayed it.

Then came that Sunday morning in church. Both girls were sitting with Anna in the second pew from the front. During the organ prelude the girls were silently signing and looking reasonably content in doing so.

The prelude came to an end, and I moved to the lectern in order to begin the liturgy. For the next fifteen minutes I lost track of Melinda and Brandi, although knowing they were still there in the pew with Anna. At the appointed moment I invited all the children to come forward for the children's message. I glanced at the twosome and was delighted that they walked up, hand in hand. They took their place alongside the dozen or so others who had wandered up to sit on the steps of the chancel, just in front of the Communion Table. I welcomed all the kids and began my little lesson. While doing so, I noted that Brandi, sitting at the end of the line, was looking straight down at Melinda, who had knelt down on the floor, directly in front of her friend. She was already signing for Brandi, with fingers moving in a blur in front of Brandi's scrunched up face.

While diving into my illustrative lesson, I recall thinking to myself this was, indeed, one of the more amazing moments I had yet experienced in ministry. A young member was drawing her special friend "into the flock," ensuring she knew she belonged and she would benefit from the wondrously insightful teaching coming from the incomparable pastor yammering away in front of them. The more I droned on with whatever my topic happened to be that Sunday for those foot-shuffling pre-adolescents sitting there, the more Melinda appeared to be helping Brandi glean choice morsels from my reflections. In fact, I noticed out of the corner of my eye, it appeared that Brandi even asked a question or two for clarification, with Melinda graciously making all things clear.

In that moment I felt all was right with the world. All the congregation had to do was watch these two angels share the blessing of the moment, and they would see in them a living example of what the community of faith is meant to be.

When I had shared all of my age-appropriate wisdom with the children, I closed with a prayer. I then dismissed them to leave for the children's activity time elsewhere in the building while the adults remained for the sermon. Again hand in hand, Melinda and Brandi departed with the rest.

At the close of the service I pronounced the benediction. I walked to the rear of the sanctuary, as was my weekly routine, to greet folks as they headed home. I confess I was feeling the afterglow of that heaven-like picture of dear Melinda helping blessed Brandi capture the rich profundities of the children's message. In fact, I was looking forward to expressing my personal and pastoral gratitude to Melinda for her extraordinary care for her young companion.

Then it all exploded. Anna came through the line, her head a bit downcast when she reached the spot where I was glad-handing parishioners. Just as I was about to gush my appreciation to her for what her gifted daughter had done during the children's message, Anna looked up sheepishly. With a furrowed brow, she said, "I owe you an apology, Bob. We all do."

I had not in the least anticipated this confession. Instead, I had been prepared to pour out to her my spirit's delight. A bit bewildered, I managed to respond, "An apology?"

"Well yes, for Melinda's behavior this morning."

"Uh, I'm not sure what you're referring to, Anna."

"You know. During the children's sermon."

"Oh, you mean when Melinda was signing what I was saying to Brandi? I thought that was one of the most inspiring things I've ever seen!"

Anna stared at me, and then cracked a little smile. "Huh. You thought that's what was going on?" I nodded, now getting an odd feeling. "Well, that's definitely *not* what was going on, Bob."

"No?"

"Oh no," said Anna dramatically. "They were having an argument. It had started a few minutes earlier while they were sitting in the pew, and it carried on through the entire children's sermon. I had tried to break it up, but they started right in again as soon as they got up there." She stopped, clearly noticing the confusion on my face. "You thought they were listening to you?" I nodded dumbly. "That's pretty funny!" she chortled. With that, she squeezed my arm in a compassionate way, and started laughing. "That is really funny!" Two or three other parishioners, standing in line and close enough to hear our exchange, guffawed out loud, joining Anna in her now mounting laughter.

It took a second—well, more like five or ten seconds—before their utterly speechless pastor let the humor of the moment begin to wash over me.

Later, taking my robe off while alone in my study, I replayed the whole scenario. I recall saying aloud, "'To such as *these* belongs the Kingdom'?"

In response to which I still swear that I heard, chuckling along with Anna and the others, the divine one intone, "Oh yes, Bob. To such as these belongs my Kingdom! To such as these!" (See Matthew 19:14)

44

Shrugs

IN SOME WAY AND in some measure, *I* was as much shocked by what I had just said as were Jimmy and Bella. The two of them stood there at the end of their driveway, staring at me, for a moment speechless. This was saying something, given the intense, argumentative spiels each had unloaded in my presence over the past ten or fifteen minutes. Minutes, mind you, that had felt like hours.

Bella had called me on the phone, begging me to drive over to their home on the other side of the village. She had explained that things between Jimmy and her had finally come to a head. They were near blows, at least verbally, with respect to their marriage.

I knew the couple well. Along with their two children, both in elementary school, they had been fairly involved in the life of the congregation. I had been somewhat aware of the stresses in their marriage, though not to any great degree.

Until now.

Responding to Bella's plea that I come right over, I arrived to find the couple standing in their driveway. Their body language spoke volumes. Even as I parked and walked toward them, they were waving their arms frenetically at each other, up and down, back and forth. As I closed in on the intense row, Jimmy dramatically turned his back on Bella, arms folded, face dark with rage. "Bob," said Bella with an exaggerated sigh, "I'm so glad you've come over." She looked at Jimmy's back and declared, "We're having another one of our fights." She then put the back of her right hand up against her mouth, and gagged. "Jimmy's just told me about his other life. Another friend." She coughed a sob. "I feel so humiliated. And angry!" The last word erupted with a look of both hurt and fury on her face.

Before I could respond, Jimmy turned toward me. "Bob, she's doing it again. Like she always does. She's overreacting. She's taking things too personally. Like she always does." His face matched hers, with the same disturbing mix of hurt and fury.

"Jimmy. Bella." I looked them both in the eye, standing now only an arm's distance from each. "Thank you for asking me to come over, Bella. Jimmy, were you aware of her call?"

Jimmy nodded *yes* and said, "I'm glad you came over, Bob. We need help." Then nodding over his shoulder toward his wife, to whom his back was still turned, he said, "She has expectations. Demands. I can't meet them all. I've never been able to meet them all." He now began to tear up. "I've never measured up in her eyes." Then he said bitterly, "I can't take it. I can't anymore."

He turned to face me full on. There we stood in triangulated formation. I invited each to explain what he and she felt was happening. For the better part of ten or fifteen minutes they unloaded about the other. It struck me that their attacks were well honed—well practiced, quite frankly. Each described in brutal detail the shortcomings and failings embodied by the other.

As they spun out their stories, however, it struck me that neither of them made mention of their two children. It was as if that twosome was purely incidental to the lives of their feuding parents. When finally each of them came to something of a stopping point in their case-making, I asked them, "How about the kids? How are they doing at this point?"

To my utter dismay, Jimmy and Bella both shrugged, almost in bodily synchrony. "They're fine," said Bella.

"They're okay, I guess," said Jimmy.

I stared at each of them, then glanced at the front of their house. There, in the window of one of the upstairs bedrooms, was a small face, peeking from behind a curtain. As soon as the child noticed me looking up at him, the curtain fell back in place, obscuring the onlooker. The moment tore at my heart. "Have you talked with them? Do they understand what's going on with the two of you?"

A chill ran down my back as I watched Jimmy give a slight wave of his left hand toward the house, saying, "Yeah, they probably know. But whatever."

But *whatever*?

I looked Jimmy in the eye, for a moment not knowing what to say. I then looked at Bella, who asked, "Do you see, Bob? Do you see what I have to put up with?"

That was when I said it. "You know what? As much as I hurt for each of you with what you apparently are going through in your marriage, I feel a thousand times more for your children. In fact, I couldn't give a rip about either of you at this moment compared to how I'm feeling about your kids."

In some way and in some measure, *I* was as much shocked by what I had just said as were Jimmy and Bella. They stood there in the driveway, staring at me, for a moment speechless. I kicked at a pebble, then continued. "If I'm going to stay and participate any further with you at this point in time, I need you to understand that at some level it's the well-being of your children that I'm concerned with." They both looked down at the pavement, silent. "I hurt for both of you. For each of you. And I have no reason to doubt that each of you feels deeply like the injured party in your marriage. I'm sorry for both of you. Believe me, I am." I stopped for a moment, collecting myself, and then said, "But as much as I'm concerned about you, I'm far, far more concerned that you keep your children uppermost in your minds. Uppermost in your arguments. Uppermost in your decision-making. Anything less than that is simply wrong." They both remained silent. But then each looked up from the pavement and quietly nodded at me.

I wish I could describe how good things came from their subsequent conversations, continuing for a bit on the driveway that day, as well as on several occasions, including in my presence, in the days that followed. But I can't. Within a handful of weeks Jimmy had moved out, leaving his two children behind in a shambles of a home. His new residence was with a friend, with whom he swore to me he had not been having an affair earlier.

In the meantime, the children remained, paying the price for parents who were so drawn into battle with each other on that driveway that they had managed only a shrug when I had asked about their children.

Over the years I've replayed in my mind—and in my soul—that whole scene. I've beaten myself up over my brazen disclosure to Jimmy and Bella that, to a real degree, I truly didn't care a whit about them in their fractious state in comparison to the intense empathy I felt on behalf of their victimized children. At one level I certainly understand children of separation and divorce are oftentimes safer, both emotionally and physically, once their parents no longer are living and doing battle with each other. But at another level, I find myself clearly inclined to be an advocate for children whose parents all too easily relegate them to upstairs windows, shrugging a *whatever* about them.

How profoundly grateful I am that our maker, our divine parent, never shrugs.

45

Snowfall Smile

I said silently to myself, "They have got to be kidding." More subtly I said aloud, "Are you sure?" The young woman and man sat comfortably on the couch in my study, holding hands and smiling shyly as so many other engaged couples had over previous years. We were spending a bit of time getting acquainted. They had come to begin consideration of the wedding they were asking me to officiate in six months, on the Saturday of Thanksgiving weekend.

They were a charming couple, clearly very bright. He was in marketing. She was a special needs teacher. It had seemed apparent they were careful planners by nature, describing to me in brief some of their dreams about home, family, and vocation.

But then that moment came when I quickly began to question my first assessment of their judgment. I listened in silence as Marlene announced, "We've decided to have the service out doors, late in the afternoon." She smiled, glanced at Darrell, and then looked boldly right at me. I didn't get the sense that she was looking for my counsel or agreement. Their decision had clearly been made. I was simply being brought on board.

"They have got to be kidding." The words jangled around my frontal cortex. But instead of blurting them out for all three of us to hear, I said in a pastoral manner, "Are you sure?"

"Yes. We're sure." Close quote, end of response.

I thought, "You asked her, Bob. Deal with it." That's when I did the clergy two-step. "So, outside, late in the afternoon, when it's already dark, in late November? When it's likely to be cold? And maybe snowing?" You'd think that my helpful questions would bring them back to a place of clear-headedness. You'd think that my pastoral wisdom would rule the day.

"Yes, that's right, Pastor Bob."

"Anything else you want to lob onto the battlefield, Bob?" I thought, while I said aloud, "So, outside, no matter what?"

"It'll be beautiful, Pastor Bob. It's what we want." She wore that winning smile that probably enticed all the special needs kids to fall in line and do exactly what their amazing teacher asked of them. Darrell smiled, too—I guess the way you do when you're in marketing and know a sale has been made, be it by you or to you.

I smiled, too, knowing that some things—most things?—maybe aren't meant to be controlled by a pastor, no matter how much I may want to play the role of orchestral conductor, dictating when the music starts and how it unfolds. Could it be that conductors *look* like they're in charge, but that the strings and wind, the brass and timpani are the ones who truly set the beat and make the music happen?

Well, if ever there were an opportunity to learn how to lead by getting out of the way, that Thanksgiving weekend was going to fill the bill.

Between that early-summer meeting in my study and the approach of Thanksgiving, Marlene and Darrell again presented themselves for several more pre-marriage counseling sessions. They proved to be as delightful a couple as could be. As we started to map out the logistical details of that looming Saturday evening in late November, they insisted all would be well. "If it's nasty outside, Pastor Bob, we'll be able to have the service inside at the wedding site. I just know, though, that won't be necessary." Marlene never stopped smiling.

Though the maestro in me wanted to let the oboist know her exuberant hopes might be dashed, I didn't want to suppress her youthful optimism. "Let reality do what reality does, Bob. She'll learn what she needs to learn." Or so I thought.

Thanksgiving came. So did the cold, and so did the forecast, now the object of my intense study. That Friday the full bridal party met at the wedding site for the outdoor rehearsal. In keeping with my responsibilities, I ensured that everyone knew what we would be doing twenty-four hours later if the conditions required the wedding's being moved indoors from the freezing patio. All the while Marlene smiled the way one does when one knows all will be well.

Saturday arrived. The Channel 13 weatherwoman forecast temperatures hovering around freezing, with precipitation moving in toward the latter part of the afternoon. "Well, that'll do it," I assured myself. "Marlene will come around. That warm and cheery indoor reception room overlooking the patio will be too inviting to resist."

However, half an hour before curtain the oboist informed the conductor that the concert would be outdoors. "It's going to be perfect, Pastor Bob." I shuddered, for any number of reasons. But who was I to argue? Whose evening was it, anyway? Five minutes before the appointed hour I lined up the wedding party behind a curtain, out of view of the bundled-up guests assembled in the reception room. On signal it all began. The guests flooded out through the doors, taking their seats on the darkened patio. Vivaldi's "Four Seasons"—the "Winter" movement, of course—wafted from the hidden Bose speakers. With my snow white robe covering four layers of clothing, I led the men of the wedding party outside and down the center aisle. Upon turning to face the seated guests, I watched as all five bridal attendants gracefully processed to the front.

Then it happened. Just as the bride and her peacock-proud father stepped through the door and out onto the shadow-filled patio, the first snow flake floated down, lazy, slow, and enchanting. Then more snow, airy and ethereal, reflecting the subdued light from the lamps hovering above the wedding party and the warm glow coming from the reception room nearby.

It. Was. Heaven.

I had to catch my breath. As did everyone there, except Marlene, because it was as she had envisioned it to be. It was beautiful beyond measure. When she and her father had joined the rest of the wedding party, she looked at Darrell, and they glowed. Then she looked at me, and we both smiled, because that's what she does, and that's what she invites everyone to do with her.

"How did she know?" I found myself wondering for just a moment, even while I intoned, "Dearly beloved, we are gathered here . . . "

Did she know?

Did it matter? Gifts are meant to be received with gratitude, not inspection, just as I'm now certain Marlene's cherished special needs children have come to know every single time she smiles at them in their cherished classroom.

46

Stomp

CHAOS BROKE OUT IN unbounded measure. I glanced back toward the congregation, right smack into the eyes of Pete, sitting on the aisle in the second pew. He wasn't more than ten feet away from me, nor the same distance from the exploding walnuts on the red carpet in the sanctuary. His expression said it all. "What hast thou wrought, Bob?"—or maybe something a little less biblical in style, but definitely in the same vein.

Talk about best laid sermonic plans.

It had all started with so much promise in the section of the grocery store where I hardly ever did much browsing. Five days earlier I had just finished scouting the fruit section, picking up the requisite apples just harvested at the nearby orchard. Then I saw them: walnuts piled high in a bin just beyond the pears. Normally I would wander right past the nut section without a second thought. Not this time. No, this time those walnuts practically cried out, "Take us! Use us!" I stared at the bin, and before I could argue myself out of the idea, I tore a segment from the roll of plastic bags nearby. I proceeded to count out two dozen walnuts still in their shell. "You fine fellows are in for a treat," I chuckled to myself.

Little did I know.

Come Sunday morning I invited the children forward for the weekly children's sermon. As usual during that particular school year, some fifteen kiddies streamed forward, planting themselves on the chancel steps in front of the Communion Table. Typically a lively group, they were ready to have at it with the pastor, whose weekly ventures into children's sermon-land often took them to places they'd never before explored. "Why disappoint them," I thought to myself as they looked in their endearing way in my direction. "Are any of you hungry this morning?" I started.

Fifteen hands shot up in the air, accompanied with a few, "Yeah, I am!"

"Well, I brought something for you to eat." All fifteen inspected with curiosity, as well as a little uncertainty, the brown bag clutched in my hands. "Here," I said as I opened and extended the bag, first toward the little four year old darling nearest me. "Take one." She reached into the bag and pulled out a walnut still in its shell. Smiling broadly, I then moved straight down the line, proffering God's blessings to each and every child. Less than half a minute into this promising moment all fifteen children held a hard nut in their hands. "What've you got there?" I asked them, all the while covertly reaching into the pocket of my preaching robe, probing for the nutcracker I had earlier planted there.

"Walnuts!" cried out five year old Charlie, down at the far end of the line of children.

"That's right." After a moment of silence, brilliantly designed to pre-pare everyone for the impending, illustrative moment when I would save the day with the "God's love"-nutcracker, I smartly invited all fifteen kids, "Enjoy!"

The script was designed perfectly. My plan was unimpeachable. "But Pastor Bob, we can't eat the nut because of the shell. We need a nutcracker to get it out." That was what the children were *supposed* to say. However, just as I was extracting said nutcracker from the folds of my robe, ready to illus-trate the transformative, shell-demolishing wonders of divine love, *whomp*!

My head jerked in the direction of the crashing noise, down at the far end of the line. There was Charlie, bless his creative soul, stomping down on his walnut with his Sunday-best sneakers, demolishing the shell to smithereens. Where just a moment earlier he had placed on the carpet his healthy, intact walnut, now dozens of shell husks were exploding into the air. Charlie, taking to heart his pastor's gracious offer to "enjoy," then fell to his knees and began fervently to inspect the mess for any surviving bits of the actual nut. Finding one, he proudly lifted it for all his intrigued friends to behold, and promptly devoured it with a grin that would have made even Scrooge melt.

For an instant I stood there, speechless and slack-jawed. Then "Uh, *no!*" somehow erupted from my throat. "*No!*" By then, not more than five seconds from when I had graciously invited each of them to eat to their heart's content, total chaos had erupted. Fifteen youthful, stomping legs were working their devastating magic on fifteen hapless walnuts. Francis Scott Key would have been proud for all the bombs bursting in air.

With the nutcracker now uselessly dangling from my right hand, I tried valiantly—but fruitlessly—to put a stop to the ecclesiastical demolition derby. "*No!*" I cried again, only to have my desperate plea drowned out by fifteen peals of delight, as well as howls of laughter coming from the congregation. Except from the aisle seat of the second pew, that is. There sat Pete, our dearly beloved, saintly, typically patient-beyond-measure, sexton. There he sat, watching in red-faced horror as his carefully vacuumed carpet was being seeded with hundreds—well, thousands—of bits of walnut and walnut shell. All being ground into that same carpet by the crashing feet of God's beloved, exuberant children.

Unsuccessful in my initial effort to recapture some semblance of churchly decency and order, and tumultuously assaulted by screams of juvenile delight and encores of laughter coming from throughout the sanctuary, I glanced over my shoulder at Pete. He was staring right at me, his face saying it all: "What hast thou wrought, Bob?" What, indeed.

Years later, I still veer away from the nut section in every grocery store.

47

Loved

IT SHOULD NOT HAVE surprised me that a simple question was all it took. It shouldn't have surprised, since questions have always sparked "aha" moments for me. "Aha" moments when I've immediately recognized within myself that which has been there all along, but which I've been somehow slow to see. Or even too preoccupied to acknowledge.

"Bob, what do you *really* think we're all supposed to believe?" Annette looked me square in the pastoral eye as she posed her question out of the blue. Our paths had crossed in the church building, mid-week. Apart from the two of us no one was around, which meant that her question was not one to be dodged, at least not in this moment and place.

Annette and I were, and remain, dear friends. Over the previous two decades we had together walked through some very trying times, both for her and for me. The gift she repeatedly gave to me, faithfully, was an undiluted honesty about her own faith-confusion. About her uncertainty, if not her rejection, concerning most things traditionally Christian. On any number of previous occasions we had discussed at somewhat numbing length the fundamental questions of the religious enterprise: Why is there suffering? Where is God—if God even exists—in the midst of that suffering?

163

Why does it appear unarguably that God permits oppression of the most vulnerable, oftentimes at the hand of the most powerful?

She and I had grappled at exhausting length, agreeing more often than not that so-called "answers" to these ageless and grating questions are not answers at all, at least to the extent of relieving us of the unsettling nature of those questions.

But then came that simple query Annette had every right, if not responsibility, to pose to her pastor and friend. "Bob, what do you *really* think we're all supposed to believe?" Some might have called the question "loaded." She might have been accusable, in the eyes of others in our congregation, of asking this question in order somehow to trap, or at least to trip up, her pastor.

But that wasn't the case in the least. Annette was, and still is, a searcher of the most honest sort. She really wonders. She truly wonders what she is "supposed to believe," at least from the institutional church's perspective. Her question was fair, sincere, and incontestably invitational, rather than manipulatively entrapping.

Knowing just that, I allowed myself a period of silence prior to answering, trusting in her innate graciousness to allow me to say whatever my heart, rather than my brain, saw fit to say. "I believe we are meant to know we are loved." I stopped.

"Anything else, Bob?" Annette asked gently.

"I believe that everything else—everything—is just details. I believe God yearns that we each know we are loved, unconditionally, boundlessly, eternally."

"Huh," said Annette. "I would have guessed that's what you'd say." I looked at her quizzically. "That's what you've been saying from the pulpit for years, Bob."

Oh.

Or more to the point: Aha.

She was right, I had to confess, or even to celebrate.

As steeped as I am in trademark theological doctrines of the reformed Protestant tradition—

As steeped as I am in well-honed explanations about God, about humanity, about salvation—

As steeped as I am in formulaic interpretations of the nature of corporate sin and elective redemption—

As steeped as I am in things ecclesiastical and intellectual, what Annette's timely question instantaneously prompted from me was a confessional honesty that what *really* matters to me has to do with love. With
knowing, in the bone of our bones and the heart of our hearts, we are the
object, each and every one of us, of divine affection. Of a love like that
of every human parent at the first glimpse and embrace of their newborn
child. Of a love that is hopelessly committed, no matter what, to being there
for and with us forever.

Annette and I remained silent for a moment. An eternity, maybe?
"Well," I finally said, "if that's what you've been hearing me say from the
pulpit all these years, I'm grateful for the privilege of preaching it, and for
being with sisters and brothers like you who have allowed me to do so."

Our conversation on that occasion, interestingly, ended far more
quickly than so many previous ones. Maybe, in retrospect, it ended quickly
for the simple fact that all the other questions, unanswered or unanswerable, simply took a rightful back seat for the moment.

Love will do that, sometimes. Love will do that, maybe for ever.

48

Relevance

IT WASN'T JUST WARM, it was hot—the way only July can be in upstate New York. A day earlier everyone had celebrated Independence Day with parades and fireworks. Now present for Sunday worship were a hearty collection of the faithful, each and all trying to sit as still as possible while the upright fans' heads wheeled back and forth, throwing some weak semblance of cool-down from each of the four corners of the sanctuary.

We were midway through the worship hour, having sung the hymn that preceded the reading of the scriptural text. I had then offered a short prayer, asking the God of true liberty to enable us to listen well to the Word before us. I was just three minutes into the meditation when it happened.

Rr—rrr—*rrrr—rrwwrr*! It was the tenacious, mechanical thrum of a lawn mower beginning to do its thing. Within seconds of its cacophonous eruption, the several elderly folks who weekly claimed the back two pews turned around toward to the rear doors of the sanctuary. Both doors had been hooked wide open by the ushers with the vague hope a whispered cross breeze might ease everyone's midsummer discomfort. All present, including the preacher caught midstream in my sermonic drone, recognized immediately that a neighbor whose home sits across the quiet street from the church building had decided to mow his lawn. Right smack dab in the middle of the worship service.

Facial frowns from the back pews suggested both irritation and even more hearing impediment than half an hour earlier. Not to be outdone by any old Briggs and Stratton, self-propelled, 150 cc behemoth, I quickly raised my voice. Raised my voice while attempting to speak of the quieting grace of the almighty. As I did so, straining to keep to my prepared homiletic reflections, it hit me. It hit me, though it went unspoken from the pulpit.

It hit me in that moment that an ecclesiastical Rubicon was being crossed. The church—not just our congregation, but the wider church— was now unarguably being proved to be considered entirely irrelevant to the wider culture. Not disliked. Not the object of derision, or scorn, or antipathy. Irrelevant.

I continued to deliver the message, straining to be heard by everyone over the insistent drone coming from a neighbor who apparently didn't really care, one way or the other, about the presence of Christ's Body in the midst of his community. I managed to churn my way through my manuscript. As I churned, however, a mixture of anger and despair coursed their way through my soul, even while my mind fought through to the sermon's conclusion. The anger was that our neighbor, whose children attended our Sunday school, and who himself worshiped at least monthly with the congregation, could unfathomably engage in such a seemingly discourteous intrusion on our one hour of weekly worship. But the despair? It was rooted in the jolting realization that the life of this blessed congregation, who for well more than a century had served the community in countless ways, was seen as worthy of barely a shrug. Seen as irrelevant in the worldview of a neighbor whose grass was getting a bit too shaggy.

That afternoon, long after I shed my clammy preaching robe and then sullenly partook of the family meal, I sat in my shady backyard and tried to make sense of it all. I confessed to myself I would much rather the congregation be assailed for some upstart action or disruptive advocacy, than for us to be treated as if not even there. I realized this moment had elicited for me the ecclesiastical parallel to the deep, gnawing pain endured by anyone who has ever been ignored, or who has been forgotten while in plain sight.

Then it struck me that this is the new reality. The church in our self-absorbed, stress-fractured culture is neither loved nor feared. The church is neither courted nor taunted. The church is ignored, seen as an insignificant irrelevance.

I slumped in the folding chair, oblivious to the heat, overwhelmed by the Rubicon.

Then I decided: it's time. It's time to look in the churchly mirror and urgently inquire of the one who proffers us true liberty what it is we are meant to do and to be; what it is the Christly presence in the midst of this carefree and careless age is fashioned to become under these soul-wrenching conditions; what it is we, sent *from* the culture in *to* the culture, are tasked to offer as neighbors to our neighbors; and what it is that will grab, transform, and even free our oddly self-absorbed world.

I decided it's time to confess our irrelevance and to commit ourselves to rediscovering the relevant one we are meant to embody.

49

The Kingdom Will Come Anyway

IT STARTED OUT AS a living room conversation not unlike many I had already experienced during the first two decades of parish ministry. He sat somewhat uncomfortably in his wheelchair in the living room, and I sat facing him, pen and pad in hand. On his request we were going into great detail planning for worship—his own memorial service.

He had been diagnosed with end stage cancer several months earlier, and he had evidently, and understandably, spent much time and energy picturing what that service would soon entail. We spent the better part of the afternoon in the exchange, allowing me to scribe lists of possible eulogists, hymns, and scriptural texts. By the end of the afternoon he and I were pretty well spent, but we agreed our work together was accomplished.

We took a break for a brief nap followed by a light supper. While he prepared for bed, I did the dishes and then sat quietly on the porch, awaiting the moment that would usher in the second phase of our bargain.

Earlier upon my arrival he and I had made a deal. I would, of course, assist him in the drafting of his memorial service. What pastor would object to doing so? But, departing somewhat from the normal such pastoral routine, I had said, "Under one condition." When he looked somewhat askance at me and asked what that would be, I had tearfully indicated I yearned for him to tell me what he had learned—what he had discovered over the course of his more than seven decades of fruitful life.

He had taken a moment to consider the proposed bargain and then had agreed, saying, "Of course. I'd be honored."

As it now darkened outside, he invited me into his bedroom. He was still in his wheelchair and asked for assistance as he struggled into bed. It took a bit, due to the pain the metastasis in his bones was clearly causing him. Once he was settled, covers pulled up to his chin to keep him from shivering, I said, "So, Dad, what have you learned?"

He looked me in the eye, then over my shoulder. He looked not at the wall beyond, but at something farther away, or someone within, and he said, "The Kingdom will come anyway."

That was it. He said nothing more in that first minute.

Echoing him, I finally asked, "The Kingdom will come anyway?"

He nodded, appearing to be both intensely serious and profoundly free at the same time. "Yes, the Kingdom will come anyway." Then he explained. Dad described how over the course of two decades in mission work in the Middle East, followed by two more decades of service through the wider church in North America and the Far East, he had often wondered. He had wondered what difference he had made—what lives he had touched in any kind of healing manner, what broken situations to which he had offered truly redemptive service. Then he said, "Now at the end of my life, I've learned I don't need to know the answer to those puzzling, even troubling, questions. I don't need to know whether my life has made a difference in the building of the Kingdom of God, because the Kingdom will come anyway."

He stopped and continued to look over my shoulder, out there or in here. He took my hand and said, "Bob, I've learned to be free, rather than bound up. I can be free, doing what I believe God called me to do, without being immobilized by the unanswerables. I've learned to be free, knowing that God has blessed me and even used me in some circumstances, to be part of God's work. But God does God's work in spite of what I, and you, and everyone else, may do. That makes it all right. That makes me all right."

We sat in silence, holding each other's hand. Warmly. Peacefully. Freed.

Dad passed away two weeks later.

I miss him deeply. But I celebrate with him, because clearly, at least for himself, he had figured it out. He had seen truth—the truth *who* had set him free. Because the Kingdom is coming anyway.

50

We Will See Each Other Again

IT TOOK ONLY A few times before I began to realize it. Those who were older got it, while their younger counterparts simply seemed not to.

It was the final three months prior to my official retirement date. For more than half a year I had announced, detailed, and repeated my plans to bring my pastoral relationship with the congregation to a close on the thirty-first of December. Now, with the maple leaves aflame and beginning to fall, I was making my rounds to see dozens of members and friends of the congregation for the purpose of saying a personal farewell. Those visits unfolded in a number of nursing homes and assisted living facilities, as well as included a large number of in-home conversations.

Virtually everyone I called on knew by then my retirement date was fast approaching, and my wife and I were planning on moving seven hundred miles westward to our newly purchased retirement home. With numbing repetition, both in monthly newsletters and from the pulpit, I had made a point of clearly stating to the whole church family that once retired and resettled elsewhere, I would no longer be available for traditional pastoral responsibilities and opportunities. Once gone, I was not returning, be it to assist with funerals or weddings. My successor, whoever the good Lord saw fit to call to be their next pastor, would be just that—their next pastor.

So the visits unfolded, with laughter and tears the norm. Hugs were exchanged where appropriate, and words of affection flowed in full measure. What I found myself doing in virtually every instance was also this. As the final, personal farewells were being exchanged, I quietly said, "We will see each other again. You know that, don't you?" Nothing more and nothing less. But it wasn't long before it happened. It took only a few times before I began to realize it. Those who were older got it, while their younger counterparts simply seemed not to. Almost to a man and a woman, the elderly would look me in the eye, tear up, smile, nod, and say, "Yes. We will." No more. No less. The understanding was crystal: we will, beyond this life, in the next, be reunited. We will not only see one another, but we will be part of an extraordinary gathering beyond anything we could ever now fathom.

But just as regularly as the elderly seemed immediately to share that understanding, those who were younger—at least younger than I—seemed not to get it. Their inability to make the connection was betrayed by a smiling, almost predictable response: "So you *will* be coming back to visit after all, Bob?" The look on their faces was one of surprise and delight, but it didn't match—didn't come close to mirroring—the tears, smiles, and nods of the more elderly.

I've wondered about that contrast in reactions again and again in the past few years. Each time I replay those contrasting reactions, and the jarring correlation with the ages of the reactors, I find myself unable to do anything other than to admit the obvious. I find myself affirming the simple reality that faith is somehow a mysterious vision which may be born in youth, but requires the passage of years to deepen, to broaden, and to embrace wonder.

Were I able to travel back in time to my younger years, I suspect—no, I readily admit—I too would likely have echoed my younger parishioners. I would have eagerly queried my beloved pastors, "So you *will* be coming back to visit after all?" But as the years have unfolded, and more and more dear ones have passed away and on, it's happened: I've begun to yearn for the reunion beyond this life. I've begun to recognize that while this life is wonderful, the next will overflow with joy, with restoration, with love.

We will see each other again. I know that now. I *know* that now!